FHM PRESENTS

TRUE STORIES 2

PLUS

Ladies' Confessions

Out Of The Mouths Of Babes

CARLTON

THIS IS A CARLTON BOOK

Copyright © 2004 Emap Consumer Media

This edition published by Carlton Books Limited 2004
20 Mortimer Street
London W1T 3JW

A CIP catalogue record of this book is available from the British Library

ISBN 184442 599 1

Illustrations: Beefy @ Folio, Kevin King, Robert Davies, Peter Greenwood, David Semple
Design: studioqube

Thanks to FHM's readers for all their contributions

Printed and bound in Great Britain

FHM TRUE STORIES 2

You've made such an effort with my parents over the last few days…

Couple forget baby device

While staying with my girlfriend's parents over the festive season, I helped her bathe our beautiful new-born baby daughter and put her to bed on Christmas evening. On reflection, perhaps we'd both had a little too much Yuletide cheer…

A WRIGHT, YORKSHIRE

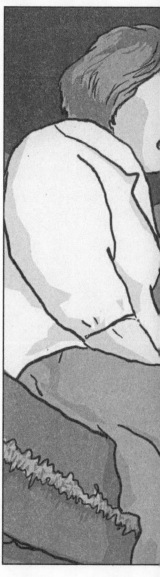

GIRLFRIEND RATTLED BY CRASH

A while back my uncle wanted to impress his girlfriend with a day out in the country, so he borrowed my dad's car – despite not being insured for it. He set off with his girlfriend… and not long into the journey dinged another car. Having no insurance details to swap he sped away from the scene of the accident, hiding the car in a field as the police cruised around, trying to find him. He managed to avoid the rozzers before finally ringing his sister to ask her to come and pick them up from the middle of the countryside. On the way home they stuck to the back roads, and his sister, enjoying all the odours nature has to offer, declared, "Wow, you can really smell that fresh country air." "No," my uncle had to correct her, "I'm afraid that's my girlfriend." She had literally shit herself from fear of being caught by the law.

K, VIA E-MAIL

LADS BLAG FOOTIE FREEBIE

A couple of seasons back, when Barnet FC were sponsored by a well-known lads' mag, it soon looked obvious that the novelty of following these football minnows was wearing off. The mag's once detailed "Barnet Updates" were becoming smaller and smaller, and it was blindingly obvious – to me, anyway – that they weren't going to the games any more. So on learning that my team – Exeter City – were playing Barnet away, some mates and I decided to take advantage of the magazine's apathy. We phoned up the London club claiming to be from the mag in question and asked to attend the Exeter game. Come the day, not only were VIP tickets waiting for us at the gate, but we were treated to a free bar, three-course meal and a round of applause from the chairman and directors at the post-match function arranged in our honour for our "unfailing support" that year. To cap off a perfect day, Exeter won.

JIM INGLE, VIA E-MAIL

Out of the mouths of babes

It'd been a hard day at work, when my colleague Michelle asked me what the time was. "4.45," I replied. "Blimey!" she said. "It was six o'clock this time yesterday."

My girl was filling in an application for holiday work. "Are you a member of a professional organisation?" asked one question. "Does that mean the IRA?" said my girlfriend.

One weekend, my sister's boyfriend announced that he intended to try out his new kite. "Don't be silly," my sister remarked, "it's too windy to fly a kite."

ASTHMATIC SUFFERS FOR THREAT

When I was at boarding school we slept in dorms. One night I awoke to the sound of ferocious movement of sheets and heavy panting to my right. Knowing that the lad in that bed was an asthmatic, I went over to check that he was okay – only to find him secreted with a torch under his sheets, having the tug of his life. When he heard me chuckling he emerged red-faced from his tent of sin with harshly whispered threats that he would kick the living crap out of me if I were to ever mention the incident. He was a big fella so I duly kept my mouth shut, and when I heard the same wheezing sounds a couple of nights later I turned over and tried to go back to sleep. Five minutes later there was a thud, and I looked up to be greeted by the sight of the big man rolling on the ground, slowly turning purple. He ended up in the medical centre, while I had a great night's kip.

GAZ, VIA E-MAIL

ANIMAL LOVER REBUFFED

Wandering home one night the worse for drink, I spotted a hedgehog in the middle of the road. Just as I was thinking that if it didn't start moving it would get flattened, a pair of headlights appeared. I ran into the road, waving frantically at the oncoming vehicle, which stopped a few feet from the poor creature, at which point I mouthed the word, "Hedgehog," and pointed at the road. The driver nodded in acknowledgement and I stepped out to rescue the errant woodland creature – until it became obvious that the hedgehog was, in fact, nothing more endangered than a U-shaped corrugated pipe from a washing machine. Not wanting to look a complete prat I pulled my sleeves over my hands to avoid being "pricked" and gingerly carried the piping to the side of the road, then nodded to the driver, who pulled away. Feeling justly miffed I then drop-kicked the pipe a good 60ft into a neighbouring garden. I should have waited a few seconds more, for the driver obviously saw me in his rear-view mirror and

Out of the mouths of babes

Playing Risk with my housemate's girlfriend, I complained about the low numbers I was getting. "Try rolling the dice one at a time," she told me in all seriousness. "That way they won't affect each other."

Watching a TV show about rhinos having their horns cut off to protect them from poachers, my lady housemate said, "That's terrible. How do they kill their prey?"

Ordering drinks on holiday, my girlfriend asked for a Margarita. I suggested getting a pitcher. "I can't," she replied, "the camera's in the apartment."

screeched to a halt, leapt out and chased me
down the road, shouting and screaming about
animal cruelty. He was beyond reason, so I ran.
So much for my good deed.

V WIGLEY, MACKWORTH, DERBY

COLD WOMAN PUNISHES VISITOR

A few winters back, a couple of mates and I were
killing time in a park when we stumbled upon
an exhibition of ice sculptures, so naturally we
had a look around. One of the sculptures was of
an attractive naked woman, which caused me to
instinctively run up to it, put my hands around
her and say, "Give us kiss, love!" before sticking
my tongue in her mouth. It was all very funny,
until I realised that my tongue had become
stuck to the freezing sculpture and I couldn't
pull myself away. My friends ran for some warm
water to part the pair of us but seemed to take
an unfeasibly long time about it, leaving me
alone to mumble incoherent excuses at dozens
of gawping park-goers.

ADAM KRAMER, LONDON

AIR-CON BETRAYAL

I'm 24 and a researcher for a car company,
which recently sent me to Singapore for some
very dull meetings about sales statistics. I went
with a female colleague whom I'd been seeing
for some time. Towards the end of the trip we
found ourselves at a table with 12 other people.
As the meeting dragged on my girlfriend kept
teasing me by running her hands down her
thighs, until I couldn't take any more.
I thumbed my phone ringtone, stepped out to
take the "call" then asked my girl to join me so
we could escape to the loo for a shag, where
I bent her over the toilets while she moaned and
talked dirty as usual. Fortified, we rejoined the
meeting… until my smug smile turned to panic
as I heard the unmistakable sound of a toilet
flush over the ventilation system above my
head. Searching the faces round the table, I met
a mix of admiration and disgust.

JON WILDING, THETFORD

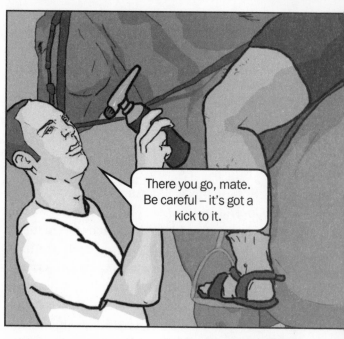

> There you go, mate. Be careful – it's got a kick to it.

Street stunt blunder

While in Malta last summer I was stripping paint off houses on a busy street while at the same time eyeing up the rather fit girls passing by. They also drew the attention of a middle-aged Maltese man with a huge belly, who was riding along on a horse. Stopping in front of me, he took out a packet of fags and asked for a light from my blowtorch in an obvious attempt to impress the girls...

CHRIS WILSON, NEWCASTLE

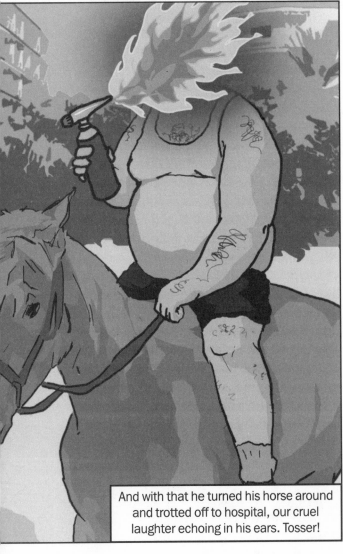

True Stories 2

PENSIONER MISSES HER TIPPLE

My uncle does his bit for society by taking the local pensioners for walks. One Sunday morning he picked up an old girl from her "retirement community". After doing the usual activities – going around the park, feeding the ducks and wandering through the markets – my uncle suggested they go back to his house, where they had lunch with his wife and two children before trooping into the front room to watch TV. The old dear asked my uncle if she could have a brandy but by the time he'd returned with the drink she was fast asleep, so he told the kids to keep it quiet while the oldie had a nice nap. A few hours later it was time to get her back to the home, but she wouldn't wake up. It turned out the family had watched the entire omnibus edition of *EastEnders* with a corpse on the sofa, while the kids, on their best behaviour, played at her feet.

KARL MATTHEWS, CROYDON

STRIPPER ASKS FOR IT

Many moons ago while on the lash in Belgium, my fellow alcoholics and I popped into a sex club. We took up position next to the stage and watched in disbelief at some of the things the fine ladies were doing to each other. One of the strippers then announced that there was the equivalent of £100 on offer to any man who would (or could) shit on her face. An eager young Belgian leapt on stage and squatted over her as she pursed her lips… but nothing happened. Another guy hopped up, dropped his trousers, and again nothing happened. While the fella next to me was explaining that if someone is blowing on your anus then you can't defecate, one of our group climbed on stage, stood over the young lady and dropped his drawers. Before she'd even had a chance to pucker up and blow, he'd emptied his load on her head. It was in her hair, her mouth, everywhere – the young chap had been suffering from the squirts for days. Our "reward" was to get chucked out. Belgians – you've got to love them.

DAVID RAMSAY, VIA E-MAIL

SOLDIER PULLS HYPER KRAUT

When I was in the Army I pulled a bird in a German nightclub. She was a little wild but I was the worse for drink, so I let her drag me back to a faceless apartment block on the outskirts of town. After drunkenly negotiating some fiendish locks on the door we headed upstairs to her flat, where we proceeded to have energetic sex well into the small hours. Next morning she was still hyper, dancing around the place, while I needed a piss, so I headed off to find the toilet. It did strike me as odd that her block had a communal bathroom and kitchen, but it was only on the way back to her room – when I passed a man dressed in white and wearing a name-badge – that I realised my companion was more than a few cards short of a full deck, and had in fact taken me back to her mental hospital.

ROBBIE BEST, NEWCASTLE

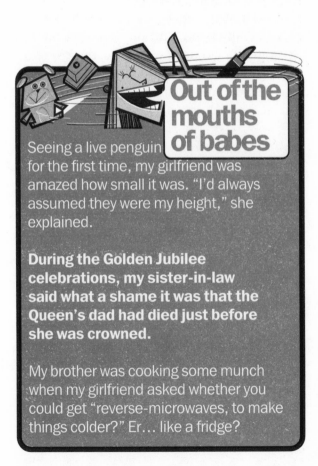

Out of the mouths of babes

Seeing a live penguin for the first time, my girlfriend was amazed how small it was. "I'd always assumed they were my height," she explained.

During the Golden Jubilee celebrations, my sister-in-law said what a shame it was that the Queen's dad had died just before she was crowned.

My brother was cooking some munch when my girlfriend asked whether you could get "reverse-microwaves, to make things colder?" Er… like a fridge?

Out of the mouths of babes

On a jolly to New Brighton, me and my good lady passed through the Mersey Tunnel from Liverpool to Birkenhead. My wife got all giddy. "This is good!" she said. "Is there one of these in Birkenhead as well?"

The missus was driving us home on the M1, northbound – except that when I glanced up from my newspaper I saw we were approaching the M25. When asked to explain why we'd gone 20 miles in the wrong direction, she sheepishly replied, "I thought we were going north because we were travelling uphill…"

CREAM TEA FOR FIDO

A few years ago when I lived with my parents I arranged a lift home with an attractive female work colleague, knowing that the house would be empty for a while. I invited her in, and before long we were going at it on the sofa in the lounge. It had been a while since my last spurt, so it didn't take long before I shot my bolt straight up her. Lying there with a smile on my face, I was disturbed to see her stand up in the middle of the room and, saying, "I hate this bit," drop my come all over my parents' rather expensive carpet. As she did this the door opened – although luckily it wasn't my parents but my pet dog, which bounded straight towards my pile and lapped it up. I quickly got rid of the lady, and five minutes later my parents duly arrived home. The first thing my mother did was sit on the sofa, to be greeted by my faithful pooch licking her all over her face.
KEVIN BLOMERLEY, WAKEFIELD

SPURNED EX THWARTED

Several months ago my girlfriend needed some bunions removed, leaving her in hospital with a huge plaster cast on her foot. I decided I'd take this opportunity to finish with her, seeing as how she couldn't really chase after me for dumping her! However, a few days later I heard a loud banging and screaming at my door. Looking out of the upstairs window I saw my ex, freshly discharged from hospital, booting the door with her heavy, plaster-encased foot. This went on until the door crashed off its hinges – but mercifully without the expected entry of a crazed harridan barking for my blood. Poking my head into the hall, I could see her lying on the porch, whimpering for help. The subsequent X-ray showed that my psycho ex had kicked the door so hard that she'd broken her right leg, leaving her in plaster for the next three months. Unsurprisingly, we're not back together.

LA HARRISON, CHESHIRE

DREAM DATE TURNS SOUR

A few months ago I got chatting to a fine young thing in the students' union, and was happily surprised when she suggested we go back to her flat. I was even more content when her flat turned out to be an overly flash-looking luxury apartment. I presumed she had wealthy parents and thought no more about it – as no sooner had my jacket hit the designer leather couch than she dropped to her knees in front of me. However, my bliss was shattered by the sound of a key in the front door, whereupon my date turned pale and told me to leg it down the fire escape. Confused and still half-pissed, I did what she said. I was halfway down the external staircase when I heard a posh woman's angry shriek from inside. "Peter!" she screamed. "It's the bloody cleaner!"

STEVO, BELFAST

There you go, mate.

G.U.M. Clinic

G.U.M. Clinic
Opening times
Mon 10.00 to 12.00
Tues 12.00 to 3.00
Weds ———
Thurs 10.00 to 12.00
Fri 12.00 to 3.00

Lad caught at clinic

Returning home after working as a holiday rep in Majorca, I started seeing my ex-girlfriend again. Sex was soon back on the agenda – but on one condition: she demanded I attend the local genito-urinary clinic to get proof I hadn't contracted any STDs. Gagging to breach her, I agreed, and asked a friend where the clinic was. He offered to give me a lift there, and I failed to smell the rat…

MGP, VIA E-MAIL

Needless to say the photo was scanned in that afternoon and e-mailed to my entire address book. It lives on even today, somewhere in cyberspace.

COSTLY CALL

Driving back from my girlfriend's one night, I spotted a police car lurking ahead. By braking sharply, I managed to get down to 30mph and cruised through without any bother. I hadn't gone more than another mile when I passed my girlfriend's dad hurtling back home well over the speed limit. Eager to earn some brownie points I called him up on his mobile to warn him of the porcine presence, but I'd scarcely exchanged pleasantries before the miserable bugger cut me off. Thinking nothing of it, I continued home. It was later that night when my girlfriend called to warn me to stay clear of the house for a while, since her dad was in a foul mood. He'd just been pulled over by the police, and although his speed wasn't too much in excess of the limit they were going to prosecute, since they saw him holding a mobile to his ear as he tootled past.

JONATHAN TINGEY, ESSEX

EGGY MISTAKE

My mum owns a cockatiel, and one day my mate and I decided to play a trick on her. Taking two white Cadbury's mini-eggs we put them in the bottom of the parrot-like bird's cage, nestling them among the ripped-up newspaper. Knowing my mum would think they were real, I was going to reach into the cage, pick out the eggs and, to her horror, scoff them down! When I returned home from work with my mate that evening, sure enough she'd discovered them, wrapping the speckled baby-birds in cotton wool. Pretending to coo over the little fellas, I plucked the "eggs" out of the cage, popped them in my mouth and crunched down hard. Out of my mouth trickled warm, sticky egg yolk. After I'd yakked up over the kitchen floor, my mate managed to stop laughing for long enough to tell me he'd come clean to my mum, and the pair of them had swapped the fakes for freshly laid ones from the breeder.

AARON HILLYARD, LEICESTERSHIRE

TAPED KNOB HORROR

A few years ago, when I was a virgin of 16, I went out with an older girl. My inexperience was obvious, as every time we so much as kissed I'd get a hard-on. So before our next night out I decided to wrap my snake in surgical gauze, then bound it tightly to my leg using insulating tape. Arriving at her parents' house that evening I found that her mum and dad were out, which meant we were soon swapping spit. I felt the tape straining, but holding, and was even able to smirk, cheesily, when asked, "Where is he tonight?" But with cruel irony this proved to be the occasion I was fated to go all the way. When nimble fingers tugged at my boxers, it was only her shriek of horror as she exposed my bulging, mummified member to the light that brought me back to reality. That, and her sobbing exit from the bedroom. I never heard from her again.

ROSS SMITH, PERTH

FART DOES DAMAGE

I was at work when I suffered the onset of a sudden attack of wind caused by the jacket potato and beans I'd had for supper the night before. I could tell that building up was a massive fart that would have both stunk and made an ear-splitting noise, but I was too lazy to slope off to the bogs on the next floor up. So to spare my colleagues – and my shame – I waddled off to a meeting room to release the monster. It was dark as I closed the door behind me and gratefully let rip, before reaching for the light switch. Unfortunately, my plan of hiding in there until the evil gases had dispersed was foiled: to my horror, the light revealed that one of the directors of the company was sitting in front of me, cradling her head in her hands. The poor woman suffered from migraines, and had been quietly sitting in the darkened room waiting for the pain to go away.

CHRIS RAYMENT, GREENWICH

PICS SHOW PAL UP

Some months ago a few friends and I logged on to an Internet chatroom, knowing that another mate of ours would be online at the same time. Registering as "saucysuzy19" we began chatting dirty to him and ended up getting his e-mail address. We must have made a good impression as the next day he could talk of nothing else but the previous night's conversation. Naturally, over the weeks we continued to e-mail him filthy anecdotes. This culminated in us sending him a bunch of amateur porn photos we'd found on the net while asking for some in return. The next day we duly received five pictures of our victim, fully naked, fingers up his arse and covered in his own come. Needless to say his girlfriend didn't appreciate being forwarded them; nor did another 50-odd mutual acquaintances.

TOM, NORWICH

TOURIST GETS RUNS IN PUBLIC

On a six-week summer trek with my mates around South America, all was going well until I came down with a serious case of the trots. This meant when I had to go… I had to go. Which is exactly how I felt as we were waiting for a bus in some tiny town in the middle of nowhere. The bus station's waiting room was little more than a shack with a man behind a desk, but by using a combination of lousy Spanish and frenzied sign language I managed to convey to him the fact that I needed the toilet. Badly. He grinned and pointed to a bucket in the corner of the room. Thinking this must be normal for a developing country and wracked by cramps, I got my mates to stand in front of me as I tugged at my trousers, squatted down and dumped my foul load in the bucket – to the dismay of the other travellers. I'd almost finished when a door swung open in the wall behind the bucket and a young lady emerged, revealing a sparklingly clean set of toilet facilities behind her.

LEE GILLIGAN, LIVERPOOL

PLOD'S PLOT RUNS INTO TROUBLE

I was once a copper, partnered with a character who liked to take out a car on night patrol on his own – meaning that after the pubs had kicked out I wouldn't see him again until 6am. We had to patrol 60 miles every night and my colleague always came back with at least 70 on the clock, but no-one could work out where he'd been – until one night, when I was told a police car had crashed on a local estate. I drove over and there was my colleague's vehicle poking out from a garage wall. It transpired that he'd taken to "patrolling" a local lady's bedroom, parking the police car in her garage, jacking the front wheels up and then, with great skill, placing the car in first gear and delicately balancing a brick on the accelerator. This allowed him to satisfy both her and the Chief Inspector's mileage targets – until some local kids had sneaked in and given the car a push. The rest was history, as was his career.
JACKO, ST IVES

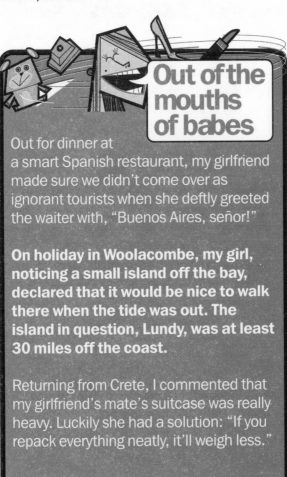

Out of the mouths of babes

Out for dinner at a smart Spanish restaurant, my girlfriend made sure we didn't come over as ignorant tourists when she deftly greeted the waiter with, "Buenos Aires, señor!"

On holiday in Woolacombe, my girl, noticing a small island off the bay, declared that it would be nice to walk there when the tide was out. The island in question, Lundy, was at least 30 miles off the coast.

Returning from Crete, I commented that my girlfriend's mate's suitcase was really heavy. Luckily she had a solution: "If you repack everything neatly, it'll weigh less."

"Chris had to lick it all off before he could leave the stage, while we took pictures. The stripper was loving it!"

Polaroid of truth

On a boys' holiday to Majorca, out on the lash every night, we heard of a gorgeous stripper called Sexy Diana appearing at a nearby bar. Naturally we went there and she was indeed the bollocks, stripping absolutely starkers on stage then calling for volunteers. Up stepped one of our boys – Chris – and she got him to lie down then smeared fresh cream over her most personal parts…

J LEVERMORE, CLACTON

"It was a couple of nights later when the owner of another bar asked to see the photos…"

That's Diana! It must be four years since he had his sex-change operation.

IMPROVISER LOSES APPETITE

I was lucky enough to have a one-night stand with a pretty foxy girl a few years back. I was busily doing said lady from behind when she screamed for me to screw her harder. I suggested a bit of bum sex but she said she didn't have any KY, so in a flash of inspiration I went to the fridge and grabbed a tub of Utterly Butterly. Back in bed I smeared a generous handful round her ring, realised it was a little too much and scooped the excess back into the pot. After a most pleasurable time I awoke the next morning to find my "date" eating breakfast: toast and Utterly Butterly. For some reason I didn't feel very hungry after that.

BAGGY, HOHNE, GERMANY

FIDDLER CAUGHT OUT

I recently drew the short straw of being the only person in my department to have to work on a Bank Holiday, but at least I'd be able to fulfill an ambition: to knock one out while sat at my desk. The only danger was a nearby ladies' toilet – there were several women working at the other end of the building. However, confident that I'd spot any ladies heading towards me in plenty of time, I called up a porn website and started stroking. Unfortunately, my meticulous planning had failed to take into account a second entrance to the toilet, and just as I got to the vinegar strokes a sneaky little minx burst out of the entrance by my desk. I span around in my chair to hide my shame, but this movement and the added excitement of a female in close proximity meant I shot my load under the desk, leaving man-paste dripping down my manager's PC. Next day it became obvious my jizz had completely screwed his CD-drive. I then watched in great amusement as Systems chided him for spilling paper glue on it, then downgraded his replacement machine.

DAVE, VIA E-MAIL

While driving to work, my partner looked out at the local school's all-weather hockey pitch, before turning to me and asking, "How often do you have to cut Astroturf?"

Watching an ad for Appletise, the missus piped up with, "I like Appletise, but it would be so much nicer if there was a non-fizzy version." That'll be apple juice.

Watching *Big Brother* with a female friend, we wondered where Cameron came from. I said he was from the Outer Hebrides. "Aren't they in space?" she said, puzzled.

GORILLA GAFFE

In an attempt to ease my student overdraft I spent some time working behind the bar of one of the seediest pubs in Yorkshire, where they employed no fewer than three gorilla-like doormen in an attempt to contain the inevitable violence. Every Wednesday, however, was "Ladies' Night" – a happy event during which anyone was capable of pulling. At the end of one such evening, while clearing up the broken bottles and glasses, I noticed a single female sat alone in the corner of the pub, her back towards me. Armed with my dustpan I ambled over to check the lonesome lady out, then swaggered to where the bouncers were comparing tattoos and declared that it was no surprise she was on her own as she was rough as a badger's arse and twice as ugly. "That's my fucking wife," one of the Neanderthals informed me. Which concluded my last night at that establishment.

ANTHONY BROOKES, VIA E-MAIL

PLOD TAKE THEIR TIME

After a night out, my mates and I were walking past a theatre when we noticed the name of the play was spelled out in large metal letters hanging on wires. Scrambling up, I managed to change The Town Mouse And The Country Mouse into the highly imaginative "wAnCer". Admiring our work, we were interrupted by some coppers. They were hardly able to disguise their amusement as they pointed out the town's biggest police station a few feet away, from where they'd watched the entire episode. Can I also take this opportunity to add that I would have got clean away as the ringleader were it not for my mate, Danny, who squealed like a pig the second his collar was felt? Thank you.

NEIL, VIA E-MAIL

Out of the mouths of babes

The other day at the fast-food outlet where I work, one of the girls washed her hands then asked with a puzzled look, "How come these driers never run out of air? Have we received some on delivery?"

Walking with my girlfriend along the seafront the other day, she came over all moody. "When I was a kid, this beach seemed huge," she reminisced. I had to spoil her musings by pointing out that the tide was in.

Taking my wife fishing for the first time, I had no bites at all – so she decided to have a go. Minutes later she was reeling in a 3 1/2lb trout. "Aren't they supposed to be dead when you catch them?" she screamed, then watched horrified as I beat its little head in with a hammer. That was her final angling experience.

SHUFFLE IN THE SPOTLIGHT

Picture the scene: one night during the Gulf War ceasefire I was stuck on a hill in a trench overlooking Dohuk, a shitty northern Iraqi city, periodically using a night-vision device to check what was going on. After a couple of hours of bugger all, my mind wandered to dirty thoughts. Needless to say the old man started to grow, and soon I was getting rid of some "pent-up aggression". The trench was cramped but as it was pitch black, I stood up and continued merrily shuffling away. Lost in thoughts of ecstasy, I disregarded two thumps from our rear lines. Seconds later the earth literally shook as an A6 Intruder flew mere feet above my position and dropped an aerial flare over the city, and two artillery shells popped out flares of their own (this was the noise I'd heard). I'd carefully timed my self-pleasuring to coincide with an Anglo-US harassment operation, which left me silhouetted and highly visible for miles around, cock in hand.

LJ, CUMBRIA

BETRAYED BY THE BOX

Having just purchased a new widescreen TV, I had a flash of brilliance in the bath: sell my old one online. Composing a description while soaking, I excitedly towelled off and ran downstairs to take a digital photo of my old telly, then e-mailed the description and picture to an online auction site. It was only when I checked the site the following day that I realised the camera's lens had picked out an item that wasn't included in the sale: me – or more accurately my plums – poking out from under a towel, perfectly reflected in the TV screen. Bids had already been placed, which meant that try as I might, I couldn't remove the photo from the site. Consequently my love-spuds were exposed to millions of internet users for a whole week. At least I sold the telly.

DAVE HARDING, DERBY

"With visions of untold gratitude and the words 'hero sandwich' firmly etched in my mind, I decided to confront the trespassers…"

Vigilante metes out 'justice'

After a spate of burglaries in my neighbourhood, I was being extra vigilant – to the point of paranoia. Which is why, one evening, after an afternoon on the sauce, I noticed my next-door neighbours' front door was wide open. My neighbours were two very lovely nurses who worked nights. Then I noticed a flickering light moving through their house…

PHIL MARSHALL, SHEFFIELD

REMOVAL MAN RUSHES IN

I used to work for a removals company, and the first – come to think of it, the only – rule we had was never to use the customer's toilet. After a particularly heavy night on the lash, however, the tortoise was showing his head just an hour into my starting a job. The car belonging to the family we were moving had disappeared from the drive, so I took a chance and dashed up the stairs four at a time, flung open the door to the loo, spun round and dropped my trousers. There immediately erupted from my arse a thunderous fart, closely pursued by the smelliest cow-pat I had ever laid. As I sat, head in hands, groaning softly to myself, I looked up to see the lady of the house standing in the shower cubicle with a bottle of bathroom cleaner, studiously staring at the tiling. Similarly avoiding eye contact I said that I'd better go, and she could only give a little nod and whimper, "Yes." I didn't venture from the back of the van for the rest of the day.

PAUL SMITH, COLCHESTER

Out of the mouths of babes

While I was driving our admittedly filthy motor past a car-wash, my fiancée decided that enough was enough and demanded I put it through the "dishwasher". Then, on realising her mistake, she told me never to send her *faux pas* "to MFI". No problem.

We were having a barbecue in our friend Cathy's back garden, and the wind was blowing smoke into the kitchen. "Can't you turn the barbie around?" asked Cathy. "Then the smoke would blow the other way."

LUCKY MOG

My girlfriend used to tell me that it was disgusting I let my cat Valentino lie in bed with me, under the covers. "What's the worst that could happen?" I would scoff. Then I found out. One night I was nodding off to sleep, the cat under the sheets, me stroking her, when I came across a hard lump on her fur. It felt like something tangled in her pelt, so I picked at it. The cat didn't mind, so I continued till I'd got most of it away. Pleased to have done my moggy a favour, it was only then I realised I'd been picking dried lumps of shit from my pet's arse.
RICHARD GORMLEY, BALLYMENA

DOUBLE THE FUN

One night at uni the lads and I stopped off at the bar to take in a few beers before going to a Man City match. Some girls we knew were there too, and we wasted no time in chatting them up. I ended up going back to one of their places, ditching the lads. We were soon up in her attic room and at it like the clappers. After various positions she wanted to do it doggy-style and I kindly obliged, but the sloping ceiling over the bed was so low that I had to open the skylight to put my head through. To my delight I discovered that her house was next to Maine Road, and I could see the pitch. So I managed to watch most of the second half, while she got the longest-lasting screw of her life.
PAUL MCLOGHLIN, VIA E-MAIL

OLDIE GIFT SPURNED

My friend is an ambulance driver, transporting the old and infirm to hospital. When management informed them that receiving a gift could lead to dismissal my friend had to tell one of his regulars that he could no longer accept her regular bags of Brazil nuts. Afterwards, the oldster's daughter cornered my mate and explained that her mother couldn't get out on her own, but that every week she brought her a selection of chocolate-covered Brazils. For months, the toothless old bat had been sucking off the choc, bagging the nuts and feeding them to my mate.
GARETH, NEWPORT

GIRL REGRETS CLUB ENCOUNTER

For a time I worked in a genito-urinary clinic in Glasgow where the patients were mostly young people, so it was no surprise to recognise them in pubs or on the street. Typically they would cross the road or hide in embarrassment – an understandable reaction given that I knew the most intimate details of their sexual escapades, and most likely had probed, prodded and swabbed their genitalia. One night I was with some friends in a nightclub when the girl next to me at the bar started chatting away like we were long-lost friends. It was clear that she recognised me, but had no idea from where. I couldn't resist stringing her along for the best part of ten minutes before the inevitable look of horror spread over her face – as she realised I'd frozen her labial warts just two months previously.
"DR" G, EDINBURGH

PEAR-SHAPED END TO POSH NIGHT OUT

When a classy girl at work agreed to go out with me, I knew she had expensive tastes, so I decided to go all out to impress her with a meal in a swanky Italian restaurant and by dressing in my best gear. I had a suit but the problem was that I didn't have a decent tie. However, after phoning a few friends I got a loan of one of those clip-on Homer Simpson jobs. The big night arrived and the meal went amazingly well. She drank loads and started to get frisky, before suggesting that I walk her home – she had her own place on the lower floor of a larger house. The journey back was fast and flirty, and when we got back to her flat she started down the steps, then turned and gave me a passionate kiss. Just like the movies, she next grabbed me by my tie and said in a sexy voice, "Are you coming in?" Needless to say the clip-on immediately came away in her hands, and she sailed backwards down the steps. A long night in A&E waiting to be seen for a badly bruised ankle killed any remaining passion left in the poor girl.
ALAN GODFREY, GODSTONE, SURREY

COPPER CRACKS CASE

Fifteen years ago I was a fresh-faced sprog straight out of police training college, sent to check on an old dear who hadn't been seen for a couple of days. There were milk bottles on the doorstep and unopened post piling up on the welcome mat so, suspecting the worst, I took my size tens to the door and started searching the house. The only room I couldn't get access to was the khazi, so once again I put my Doc Marten's to work. The door flew in then immediately bounced back, hitting me in the face. Opening it a little more carefully this time I entered the room, to find that the poor old lady had obviously died of a heart attack while laying a log, fallen off the shitter and blocked the door with her head. She now also had a nice big dent between the eyes, courtesy of yours truly – a fact I tactfully omitted on returning to the nick to submit my report. Turning up the next day, I had a bit of a shock when I found that a murder incident room had been set up for an old dear whose post-mortem revealed a fractured skull. It was a very nervous young copper who gave a rather more detailed report to the detective superintendent later that morning…
PAUL, VIA E-MAIL

Finding myself alone for a minute, I craftily emptied my glass into the hearth, intending to follow up with a beer.

Cocktail dodger gets just reward

Every Christmas Eve, my ex-girlfriend's parents would host a family get-together. Naturally, I was always forced to attend – until one festive evening. The event was taking its usual course, and the time had come for her dad to grandly serve his "Christmas Cracker" – an appalling cocktail tasting like a mix of Grand Marnier and lighter fuel…

MARK ADAMS, LONDON

My singed eyebrows were ignored as the decorations went up like Dresden. That was my final Christmas Eve invite...

PET BETRAYS PETTING

Some time ago I was sort-of seeing a girl I'd met in Tenerife that summer. I say "sort-of" because she was engaged at the time, which meant the only way we could get together was when she was able to make an excuse to her hubby-to-be and hotfoot it across town. As I was still living with my parents, we'd go for a hefty piss-up while waiting for my folks to go to bed, then use the front room as a make-do shag shack and ride the night away. After one of her hasty early-morning departures, my conquest phoned to say she'd lost her knickers and a sock; eager to avoid an embarrassing confrontation with my mum I turned the front room upside down, but couldn't find the missing garments anywhere. Until later, that is, when a pleasant evening's family television viewing was interrupted by my parents' puppy staggering into the lounge and vomiting a black G-string onto the living-room rug. I never did find the sock.

SIMON CLARK, LOWER KINGSWOOD

BALL DARE BACKFIRES

When I was a 14-year-old at boarding school, lights out in the dorm was the cue for a whole bunch of arsing around. One incident involved a game of dare, during which my mate Dave bet he could fit both nads into a Marmite jar. Such a receptacle was produced and Dave soon proved the doubters wrong but, unfortunately, he couldn't extract his testicles. He then walked around for two days with his love-nuts trapped in glassware, before desperation drove him to the design workshop. His plan was to remove the jar by smashing it with a hammer: a foolhardy procedure that resulted in him smacking one plum square-on and cutting the other with broken glass. He lost the bruised bollock and, on visiting him in hospital, I was sworn to secrecy – a vow I have maintained ever since. Er, until now.

PHIL MARSH, SEVENOAKS

SHOPPING TRIP TURNS SOUR

After a stint working offshore as a welder I gratefully boarded the train from Aberdeen, and proceeded to celebrate my return to dry land with a few beers. Consequently, I soon felt the need to relieve a little gaseous pressure. The carriage was quite full so I cocked my leg and tried to sneak out a quiet one – but disaster struck and I followed through. I could feel the parcel wedged in my crack, so at Edinburgh I gingerly de-trained and went to a shopping precinct, found a clothes shop and hurriedly bought the first size 38 denims I could find, before waddling back to catch the next train. As soon as the train was moving I dived into the toilet, ripped off my old jeans and skiddies and tossed them out of the window. After cleaning myself up I opened the package I'd bought, to find… a Wrangler jacket.
MIKE, NEWCASTLE

Out of the mouths of babes

Listening to a report on the radio about the summer solstice, my girlfriend Lucy asked, "What's the solstice got to do with druids? Aren't they those little robots out of Star Wars?"

After constant nagging, I bought my wife a breadmaker. Eyeing the instructions, she turned to me in disappointment and said, "I didn't realise it needed ingredients as well." Silly me – I'd only gone and bought the non-magic version.

Surprised to read that raindrops only fall at 7mph, I wanted to know what my girlfriend would guess. "They come down from quite high…" she mused, "so maybe a few thousand miles per second?"

True Stories 2

Out of the mouths of babes

Supermarket shopping with my beautiful girlfriend, I asked her to grab a pack of medium fresh eggs. With no response I turned to see her staring puzzled at the shelves. "Can't we just get some fully fresh ones?" she asked.

One night the electricity went off. "It's definitely a power cut," I told the missus, looking out at the street in blackness. "It can't be," she informed me. "All the passing cars still have their lights on."

A news report said how they were going to stop servicing the Hubble Space Telescope after 14 years in orbit. "Does that mean the astronauts on board can finally come home?" asked the girlfriend. She's studying to be a doctor.

TILE MAN CAN'T COMPLAIN

When I worked for a company selling tiles and bathroom suites, a woman a few years my senior came into the showroom for the umpteenth time having finally decided on the tiles she wanted. As on her many previous visits she flirted like mad with me, bending over as I loaded up the car so I could see the tiny thong she was wearing. Consequently, as an act of sheer chivalry, I offered to ride with her and unload the tiles back at her place. The conversation on the drive back was awash with innuendo, so it was no surprise when my fourth tile-laden journey up the stairs was interrupted by the bedroom door opening – and her inside, wearing nothing but the thong. Before I knew it I was getting the ride of my life! Unfortunately, when we were done, I still had to finish unloading the car. Being understandably knackered, on my next haul I slipped on the bathroom mat and tipped a box of tiles into the bath, leaving it with a massive crack. So we ended up going back to the shop, which meant that not only did I get the shag of a lifetime but commission on the sale of a new bath. Result!

PAUL ASHTON, GLASGOW

CHUNDERER'S CHUCK LIVES ON

As a fresh-faced first-year at uni, I went on a night out with my new housemates. When we got back to our top-floor flat I was battered, so after polishing off a take-away I stumbled to bed. An hour later I awoke, needing to be sick. However, I could hear my new chums chatting in the living room and I'd have to pass them to get to the lav. So, to save face I stood on my bed, prised the top of the window down and spewed my guts out. Brilliant! Except that next morning I was greeted by a pebble-dashed pane and window ledge, stinking and impossible to clean. That wasn't the end of it, as the next day I was awakened by a knocking sound. For a week this continued until I opened the curtains quickly enough to expose the culprit: a cheeky magpie, happily chipping away at my crusty chunder.

JC KAY, LEEDS

FACE-CLOTH FAUX PAS

After a night out with pals, I decided to call in on my then-girlfriend for a bit of late-night lovin'. Having quaffed a few bevvies, I slept like a log – until the early hours of the morning, when I woke up with a banging headache. The only immediate cure I could think of was something cold on my forehead, so I stumbled groggily into the bathroom, grabbed the first flannel I could find and stuck it under the tap. I then returned to bed and comforted myself by draping the cloth on my face, enjoying its moist dampness… until I was woken by a shriek from my girl. "What's that doing in here?" she screamed, pointing at the flannel. I soon found that the thing I'd used to soothe my face was in fact her mum's "special cloth" – the fanny flannel she used to wash her muffin. Not the best start to the day, believe me.

JAMES, PRESTON

For several nervous miles we proceeded along country roads to the crematorium.

Funeral shunt

The impact had buckled the rear door, and bungee ropes were needed to preserve what was left of my poor old gran's dignity.

After somehow managing to scrape through my driving test a few years back, I "invested" in an F-reg Ford Escort. Not long after passing the test my grandmother died, and I was volunteered to chauffeur family members as part of the funeral. Come the sad day, I was alarmed to see the funeral director plonk one of those black magnetic cones on the nose of my knackered motor. He then gestured for me to head the parade of private cars and follow his limo, itself directly behind the hearse with the old girl's coffin in it...

DAVE WILSON, CHESTERFIELD

Seeing an empty roundabout approaching I drove straight on. The two cars ahead, however, had stopped...

The family laugh about it now. Several years later.

True Stories 2

DRINKER RUES NAP

Following an afternoon's drinking, I decided I'd reached my limit at 6pm and tottered off to the bus stop for the 30-minute journey home. Unfortunately, the combination of lager and the warm top-deck of the bus meant that I immediately fell into a drunken coma. It was a full two hours before a fellow passenger shook me awake, when I saw we were in the centre of Manchester. I stumbled off and went to the station to catch a train home. To kill time I strolled round the station and picked up a paper before catching the train, eventually arriving home about 9pm. It was only 30 minutes later, after I'd taken a piss, that I finally looked in the mirror. To my horror, my nose had been covered in highlighter pen, while my forehead boasted the word "TWAT" in biro – which explains the look I'd got in the newsagent.

TONY PYE, ABBEY HEY

Out of the mouths of babes

In Paris, me and the missus went on the Ferris wheel, enabling me to point out the Eiffel Tower. "What's the other tower over there?" asked the wife – pointing at the reflection in a glass building.

Reading Out Of The Mouths Of Babes recently, my girlfriend asked, "What's 'WWII' mean?" I told her they were Roman numerals. "Were the Romans involved in World War Two?" she replied.

After a frozen car door incident, my then girlfriend bought me a can of de-icer. A few days later she came round and saw her present in the kitchen. "You should keep it in the glovebox of your car," she suggested. "Then it's always handy."

PRANKSTER REWARDED

A few years ago I worked in a bacon-processing factory. One day, tired of feeding joints of pig meat into the slicer, I decided to relieve my boredom by playing a joke on the girl working further down the conveyor belt. Letting out a scream from behind the machine, I tossed a rubber glove full of piggy off-cuts onto the production line. My high-jinks fell flat, however, when on spotting the "severed hand" my co-worker fainted, falling head-first onto the belt. As her hair wound around the pulleys I managed to hit the emergency stop button, then stuffed the glove into my overalls and shouted for help. I got the rest of the afternoon off as the fire brigade worked to release the poor girl, who luckily had no memory of what had happened. The next day I was called to the MD's office. Expecting a P45, instead the old boy heartily shook my hand and passed over a cheque for £250 as reward for my "prompt actions" which had "probably saved the girl's life".
MARK WRIGHT, THETFORD

HAIR HACKER CON

A few years ago I joined the police, which meant going to training college deep in the countryside, where we were continually hassled about our hair being too long. That was lucrative news for the local barber, who would drive to the school once a week and hack the cadets' hair for a fiver. Luckily, one of our course members was a barber before joining the force and would provide the same service at a fraction of the cost – namely his beer and smokes for the 15 weeks of our incarceration. Although he drank like a fish and smoked like an Iraqi oil well, it worked out cheaper, so every Sunday a queue would form while he trimmed our bonces into the requisite thug-like haircut. At the passing-out parade, we got to meet his wife and commented on how his skills had saved us money. Laughing, she revealed he'd never cut hair in his life. Our "barber" had, in fact, been a landscape gardener before joining up, but had wanted to try haircutting because "lawns and heads are pretty much the same".
RICK STEVENS, ABERGAVENNY

ORAL LOVER'S SURPRISE

In a bid to save some cash, my girlfriend and I once shared a room with a mate in a flat. It was cheap, but the downside was that we didn't get to spend much "quality" time together – until one fateful night when our roommate announced he wouldn't be back till dawn. The moment the door shut we stripped off our clothes and jumped straight into bed. I'd recently had my tongue pierced with a ring; my girlfriend loved for me to go down on her, so, wanting to drive her wild with my new toy, I duly obliged. Ten minutes later she started tugging at me, wanting a little more than tongue, so I began to pull myself up. But a shriek of pain came from my girl and I found I couldn't lift my head – my instrument of pleasure had become entwined in her pubes. I tried to unscrew the ring, but it was too slippery, so after much squirming we realised that pubic trimming was the only option. It was 20 agonising minutes before our flatmates vacated the kitchen and, wrapped in a duvet like some kind of high-tog mutant crab, we could shuffle downstairs to retrieve the household scissors.

SEAN MCFARLANE, VIA E-MAIL

VOMIT JEST BACKFIRES

After substantial over-indulgence in the course of a night out, my girlfriend and I returned home feeling quite sick. Being no beginner in the regurgitation stakes, I fetched a basin and left it next to the bed in case one of us needed an emergency throw-up during the night. Next morning I was first to wake up, and glancing down saw that the basin remained uncontaminated. I thought it'd be a laugh to pretend I'd been sick during the night, then throw the "vomit" over the missus. So I gave her a nudge and, when she opened her eyes, picked up the bowl and hurled its contents at her. It was then that I found out she had indeed been sick – the sort of clear-looking, watery variety I'd entirely failed to notice at the bottom of the bowl. It ended up all over her, somewhat spoiling my hilarious joke. And my sex life.

DAVID BAND, FIFE

MATE DOPES DIVER

On a diving trip to the Red Sea, my mate Trevor asked me for a "Zantac" for his heartburn. Being in a rush, I legged it down to my cabin, grabbed the pills and threw them to him. After the dive, Trev popped down to his cabin – and wasn't seen again for most of the day. As the week progressed, I began to get worried about why Trevor was so quiet – he's normally the life and soul of the party. To be honest, it got so bad that some of the females on the trip thought he was suffering from depression, as he spent most of his time alone. At the end of the week, as I packed I came across my Zantacs at the bottom of my bag. It was only at the airport, as Trevor was explaining how out of condition he must be as he'd felt completely knackered for the entire trip, I realised I'd thrown him my prescription sleeping pills that first day.
STEVE WILD, VIA E-MAIL

Out of the mouths of babes

Me and the missus noticed an old motor in a car park. "It's been there so long, it's sunk into the tarmac!" she said. It had four flat tyres.

My ex saw *The Godfather* and was halfway through the second one before asking, "Is Michael Corleone something to do with the Mafia?"

The pub conversation got round to the subject of anal sex. "I couldn't be doing with that," said my mate's girlfriend. "I'd need more than one bonk a year."

Watching a programme on turtles, my girlfriend became confused. "Are turtles born with shells on their back?" she burbled, "or do they need to find one?"

Gown blunder

My wife was ready to drop our first sprog when her waters broke at three in the morning. With her contractions getting closer and closer together I was bricking it, but worse was to come. On arrival at the hospital a nurse told us the baby was breach – it had twisted the wrong way round. Because the as-yet-unborn nipper couldn't be turned, an emergency Caesarean was required…

IAN MILLS, WHITLEY BAY

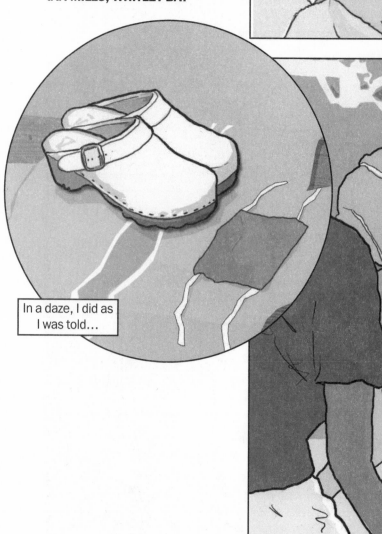

In a daze, I did as I was told…

Only after my baby was born did a laughing surgeon explain that I was supposed to wear the gown over my clothes.

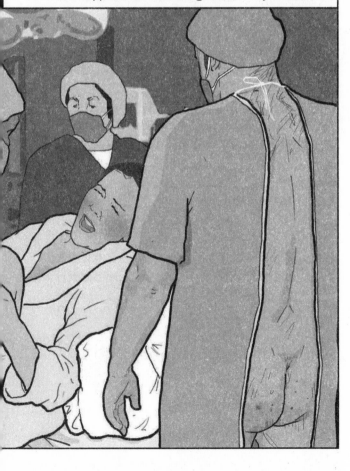

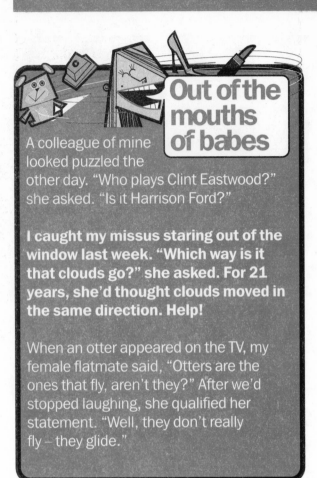

Out of the mouths of babes

A colleague of mine looked puzzled the other day. "Who plays Clint Eastwood?" she asked. "Is it Harrison Ford?"

I caught my missus staring out of the window last week. "Which way is it that clouds go?" she asked. For 21 years, she'd thought clouds moved in the same direction. Help!

When an otter appeared on the TV, my female flatmate said, "Otters are the ones that fly, aren't they?" After we'd stopped laughing, she qualified her statement. "Well, they don't really fly – they glide."

DRUNK PERFORMANCE BACKFIRES

Some years ago I dated a 17-year-old, whose parents – while not disapproving – insisted she be back by midnight. One evening, as home time approached, I persuaded my girlfriend to stay over, then phoned her mother to explain that she'd had one too many and passed out on the sofa. I went on to say that I'd drop her off next morning. Unfortunately my cunning plan backfired when her mum immediately rang off, jumped into the car and drove over to pick her up in person. That meant that to save our relationship, my girlfriend had to turn in an Oscar-worthy impression of being slaughtered. So impressive was it that Mum took one look at her little princess then marched her upstairs to my bathroom and bundled the poor lass under a cold shower, fully clothed. Curfew was strictly observed from that day onwards.
NEVILLE COPLEY, LEEDS

HUNGRY FATHER WADES IN

While I was courting I'd go to my girl's house for Sunday tea with her folks and we'd always end the meal with tiramisu. One evening, my girlfriend and I retired to her bedroom, taking our desserts to eat in front of the TV. One thing led to another and soon I had dipped my old fella into one of the bowls of gloop. Much fun ensued and within minutes I was dispensing a helping of sticky pudding of my own. Soon afterwards, I could hear the dishes being cleared downstairs, so I picked up the remaining tiramisu and walked onto the landing, to be met by my girl's dad coming up the stairs. Seeing the bowl of pud in my mitt, he said, "Not eating that?", snatched it from my grasp and to my horror began to spoon the gooey, cock-flavoured treat into his mouth. I was horrified to say the least, but he simply smiled at me and said, "Mmm, lovely!" It remains a family secret to this day.

SM, LEICESTERSHIRE

SPEEDY SQUADDIE

Some years ago, I was a young soldier serving in Belize. It was hot, humid and bloody boring – our only entertainment being wagers involving rounds of beers at Happy Hour each Friday. One of our bets was to see who could get to Punta Gorda airport the fastest. One Friday, I was on duty and got lemoned into taking my boss to the airport. It looked like a good way to win myself a free night's drinking! We were meant to leave at 10.15 for an 11.00 flight, but he kept me waiting for 20 minutes. Finally we climbed into the Land Rover and I floored it. Everything seemed to be going great on the approach and a new record looked like being in the bag – until we came to a hold-up. A bunch of kids were walking down the middle of the road, a couple of adults out in front. The boss told me to beep the horn to get them to move over, so, being a good soldier, I did as ordered. The kids finally shifted, but I drew some evil looks from them as I pulled past. It was only when I drew level with the adults that I realised I'd just forced a child's funeral procession off the road.

JIM BARRY, EAST YORKSHIRE

PUGILIST REGRETS LAST BOUT

Aged 18 I faced a dilemma: pursue my boxing career or become a doctor. Medicine won. It was six months after my last fight when I was sitting in a pub with a couple of cold drinks and got a call from my old coach, desperate and begging me to fill in for an injured fighter at a show later that very night. It was to be one of those exclusive dinner-and-boxing affairs in front of a bunch of prominent people, including the mayor of Belfast, no less. Still, despite the dazzling company I politely declined until my coach told me the name of my opponent. I detested the guy! Spurred on by the thought of having one last pop at him – and, to be honest, by the booze – I caught a cab home, dusted off my gear and an hour later was in the ring, pumped up on adrenalin and ready to go. In the first round I boxed well, bloodying my oppo's nose and humiliating him with my defensive wizardry. However, in the second he caught me flush in the stomach with a right jab. Immediately a tidal wave of half-digested Guinness gushed from my mouth, coating my opponent. Of course, the fight was promptly stopped and I exited the hall to a chorus of hysterical laughter, shame-faced, and with Guinness puke dribbling from my chin. As if that wasn't humiliation enough, it was a sound I was to hear over and over again: the bout had been filmed, and the resulting video in aid of local charities was bought and endlessly replayed by every one of my "friends".
C CAMPBELL, WARRENPOINT

STAG SLIP-UP

On a recent stag trip to Amsterdam, we all loosened our inhibitions herbal-style before migrating to the red-light district. As you do. Before long most of the group had ducked behind one scarlet curtain or another, leaving a moral majority – Dave and I – to think pure thoughts. Dave was the groom-to-be so it was no surprise that he abstained; nor was it a shock when he announced he was popping off "to get a little something for himself", as he'd already smoked his way through a forest of pot and was doubtless off to score some more weed. In his absence, the remainder of the party returned with various smug expressions on their faces. Half an hour later and with no sign of Dave, his delectable but insecure fiancée called my mobile. Was her boy all right? she wanted to know. Could she speak to him? She was asking me because the best man, Stuart, hadn't made the trip. I was running out of small talk when at last Dave reappeared, grinning like a loon. I thought it would be a laugh to have him "confess" his low-level drug abuse to his betrothed, so I shouted that Stu was on the phone and wanted to make sure he'd been a bad boy. Without a second's pause, Dave snatched the mobie and bellowed, "Stu! You'll be so proud of me! I just found the biggest, fattest prossie there is and got her to take it right up the arse! I never get that at home, and it only cost me 30 Euros! You there, Stu?" Amazingly, the wedding still went ahead. Without me.

GARY, LINCOLN

Out of the mouths of babes

Discussing fake IDs, a mate said you could get a good one via the black market. "What day's that on?" asked my girl.

After visiting the London Dungeons I told my girlfriend the story of Jack The Ripper. "Did they ever catch him?" she asked. I explained that they hadn't, but there had been many suspects. "Then he could still be wandering the streets of London today!" she gasped.

My father couldn't decide whether to sell his personalised numberplate or transfer it from his car onto his motorcycle. "Won't it stick out on either side?" chipped in my sister.

Bather gets shock

When I finally got set up in my own flat with my girlfriend, one of the first things I did was invite my younger brother round to stay for the weekend. As a treat for the boy, I'd bought him a Scalextric set, which my girl and I set up in the living room the night before he was due to arrive. After checking the cars were running, I toddled off to take a bath…

MICKEY W, SUTTON COLDFIELD

When I returned, my girlfriend had just spun the car off the circuit…

Still wet, the last thing I felt was my old fella brushing the track…

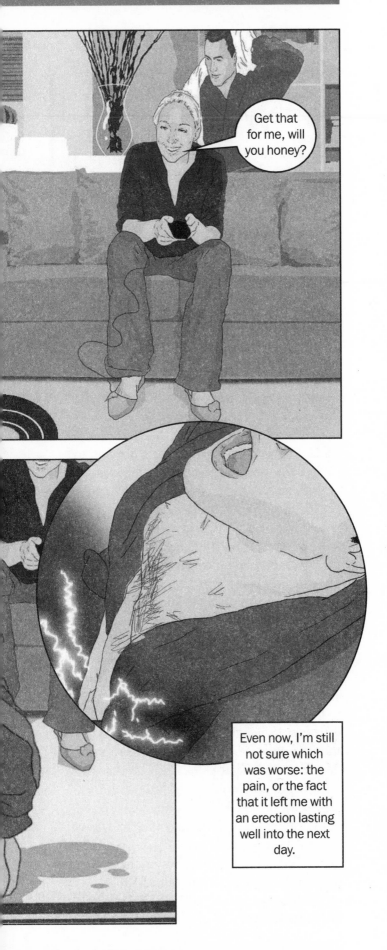

Out of the mouths of babes

On holiday, during dinner, a girl at my table pointed out that it felt like we were moving. We were on a cruise.

Watching *Who Wants To Be A Millionaire*, the question, "Which Biblical character was famed for his enormous strength?" came up. "Popeye!" exclaimed the missus.

UV BETRAYS TUGGER

I once had a girlfriend who still lived with her parents, but generously enough they'd let me crash in her room overnight. After we'd satisfied each other's sexual appetites we'd drop off to sleep, but I was a rampant young teenager then and after a quick nap I'd regularly wake up with my diamond-cutter restored. The girlfriend would be out for the count, so I got into the habit of sticking my manhood out from under the covers and slowly tugging away for anything up to an hour, before letting fly across the room onto her suitably cream-coloured carpet. By morning, all evidence of my stray loin-juice would have evaporated, so the secret of my overactive nuts remained hidden… until the day my girlfriend hired a sunbed. Her father and I lugged the thing into her bedroom and set it up under the watchful eye of her mother, who threw the switch to spark up the eight-tube monster. Like a scene out of CSI, the room was flooded with brilliant blue light – under which my army of long-abandoned little soldiers positively glowed. For a second I was flushed with pride at just how far my muck had flown over the months, until her parents got on their hands and knees, rubbing away at the carpet to try and work out what had caused those mysterious stains…

KINO, ABERDEEN

LOVER LIMBERS UP

A couple of months after getting together with an air stewardess, the hospitable lass gave me the key to her house with the freedom to pop round unannounced if my night-time urges so dictated. Clearly, her job meant she was often away for days at a time. So when she called one evening to say she'd just landed in Manchester and felt horny, I was on the road within seconds and soon letting myself in, ready for the welcome-home shag of a lifetime. Making myself at home, I "warmed up" naked on the sofa – curtains closed – with one of our Swedish videos. Sure enough, soon I heard the back door opening. My excitement quite literally grew as her footsteps approached the living room, and I threw the door open, cock in hand… to be confronted by her father, holding bread and a carton of milk. Apparently, the old boy always popped round to turn the heating on and stock up on perishables when his little girl was due back home. Thankfully he omitted any mention of the incident from the wedding speech he gave for us last month.
MARK ROE, SHEFFIELD

BAG SWITCHER

When we moved in together, my girlfriend and I soon got into a routine: each morning while I was in the shower, she'd make my sandwiches, bundle them up in a plastic carrier bag and leave them on the kitchen table for me to pick up on the way out. My workmates were most impressed at this domestic harmony, and would joke about her secreting chocolate treats and little notes in with my scran. The joking stopped one lunchtime, however, when I emptied out the bag to reveal not tasty sarnies, but a mess of waxy cotton buds, tissue paper and a single used tampon. In my haste I'd picked up the full bathroom swing-bin, which my girl had left for me to drop off in the dustbin.
S SHIPPIN, LONDON

True Stories 2

BOAST TURNS SOUR

A few years ago I worked in a bar on the north coast of Northern Ireland with my mate, Sparky. This was where we got to know a young lady who was up for the summer. In fact, the pair of us got to know her very well – by shagging her in every way possible. At the end of the summer she left to work in Canada, and that was the last we heard of her... until the following year, when a guy dropped in for a drink. He was a golfer over for the Black Bush amateur tournament, and said he'd been told about the bar by the same young lady. All it took was a vodka and Red Bull and within minutes I was boasting to this bloke about all the sordid activities Sparky and I had got up to with this girl – blow-jobs, DPs, shooting all over her face. Then I asked him how long he'd known her. "About eight months," he told me, "but we've only been engaged for the last two."
ALAN NEVIN, COLERAINE

DRIVING LESSON ENDS BADLY

A few years ago I took driving lessons during my college's summer break. When it came to the end of my fourth lesson, my driving instructor had enough confidence in my abilities to let me drive us home. As I turned into the entrance of my road, he told me to be careful of a man fixing something under his jacked-up car, his legs sticking out. I proceeded to creep down the road as another car came the opposite way. We were touching wing mirrors as we passed... then I felt a crunch under my passenger-side wheels, followed by a blood-curdling scream. My driving instructor looked out of the window, turned back to me with a face of horror and screamed, "Drive! Fast!" I barrelled it to the end of the road before asking the instructor how bad the guy looked. He couldn't tell me because he was laughing so much. Only when he managed to get himself under control did he explain that I hadn't run over the grease monkey's legs but his can of Coke, spraying it all over him.
DAVE ENGLAND, VIA E-MAIL

THIN WALLS PROVE TEMPTING

The girlfriend and I had moved into a new flat, followed a couple of weeks later by a couple downstairs, who turned out to be sex-mad – they were at it 24/7, and extremely loudly! One night I came home to find that my girlfriend had gone to visit her parents, so I flicked on the TV. Naturally, this was when my neighbours decided to have a shagging session. As they got louder and louder I decided that if you can't beat them, join them, so I went into the bedroom – which was above theirs – in order to hear better. It was actually quite a turn-on, so I lay down with my ear to the carpet and embarked on a five-knuckle shuffle. Before long, both me and them were getting to the point of no return... when the bedroom door was flung open and there stood my girlfriend with her mum and dad. She'd brought them round so they could hear how noisy the flat was. I can safely say this is the most embarrassing thing that has ever happened to me, and you can imagine the atmosphere each Sunday during dinner at her folks' place, even today.

GREG, LIVERPOOL

BEWARE THE BOT

I'd come back to Britain after leading an expedition of 16 students through the jungles of Belize. They'd been half-gnawed to death by mozzies, but I thought I'd got off lightly with just a few bites on my left eyebrow. However, within a week my eye had swollen up. Gentlemen, meet the Bot Fly. This little bastard catches a female mosquito and lays its eggs on it. The eggs drop off when the mosquito bites you, your body heat hatches them out and the larvae burrow into your skin. My local A&E had to perform surgery to extract the things, which had used backwards-pointing barbs to anchor themselves into my eyebrow flesh. End of story? Sadly, no. Three weeks later I was relaxing in a bath when I felt pressure behind my eye. I then squeezed out no less than four 2cm-long squirming maggots from my skull; one popped out so hard that it flew through the air into the bath water. Anyone want some free fishing bait?

BEN CHURCH, REDBROOK

Waiting until my parents were out, I loaded up my dad's brazier.

Having a bonfire, Markie?

Bonfire of the porno mags

I'd had my porn stash for some time and was getting bored of looking at the same old breasts and weasels. Getting a girlfriend might also have had something to do with my decision to get rid of my scuff collection. And what better send-off for it than a Viking funeral?

MARK LUNN, LEEDS

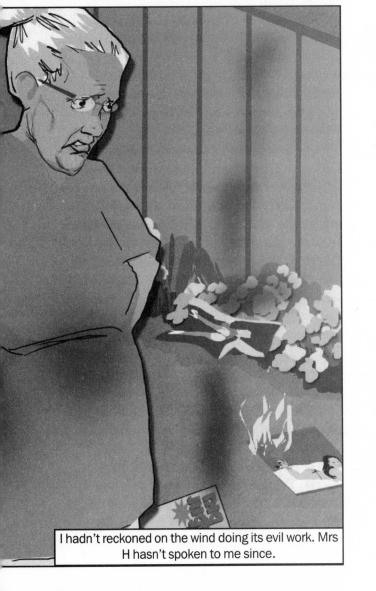

I hadn't reckoned on the wind doing its evil work. Mrs H hasn't spoken to me since.

SPANISH NOOKIE GOES AWRY

The wife and I had rented a villa with my parents, and it wasn't long before the Spanish sun began to induce its usual daytime horniness. One day, after lunch by the pool, my parents announced they were going to the local shop, giving us the perfect opportunity for some alfresco fun. The wife went on her knees under the table to perform her matrimonial duties. Mere minutes later I let my good lady know that I was about to erupt by shouting, "I'm gonna come!" The mood was somewhat spoiled by the sound of my mother saying, "Okay, we'll wait for you." My parents hadn't left yet, and were standing in the doorway to our right! Being at the point of no return I had no option but to let nature take its course. My wife, however, panicked and pulled her head back, leaving me to fly freely – only now did my parents realise what was happening. They were so disgusted that they refused to eat their lunch off the table for the rest of the holiday.
STEVE WHEELER, VIA E-MAIL

FIREMAN'S BONUS

There used to be a cul-de-sac where the local "working girls" would pose in the windows of the houses. One night our fire engine received a call to a flooding there. Sure enough, when we arrived two girls in stockings and suspenders were standing in the doorway, water pouring through the ceiling into the living room. Luckily one of the lads on the truck had worked as a plumber, and diagnosed a burst tank. With this isolated, we drained off the remaining water. Before we left, I joked with the girls that when this kind of incident occurred in a restaurant we got a free meal off-duty, or a free drink if it was a pub. What did they have to offer? To my surprise, hand-jobs for all would be available later! There were five men on that appliance and all of us swore we never went back. But a couple of years later the same house suffered a small fire. Recognising me, the girls said that the same offer was up for grabs – but hopefully more than two of us would take them up on it this time! I never did find out which two…
SAM, BIRMINGHAM

BOTTLE'S REVENGE

Driving through the American south-west with some mates, we stopped at a roadside café somewhere in the middle of the desert. After parking the car and working out a touch of deep-vein thrombosis, we spotted some bottles neatly lined up in a row against the base of a nearby wall. Naturally, we started hurling rocks at these targets. Two of the three bottles smashed really quickly, but one just wouldn't succumb from long range. In the end I reasoned that as skill hadn't prevailed, a more direct approach was required – so I found a larger rock and stood right above the bottle, then smashed the thing down. It was only after a spray of rancid liquid had flown all over my jeans and shirt that I realised the bottle had been thoughtfully deposited there by another passing motorist – judging by the smell, a couple of days ago. And what happened to my caring mates? They ran into the caff with the car keys, forcing me to walk through a throng of diners who all too obviously recognised the bitter stench of stale urine.
KYLE, BRISTOL

THE LUCK OF THE IRISH

I was at a house party in Dublin and, as we Irish do, had consumed copious pints of the black stuff before arriving. The house was jammed, and I very quickly proceeded to chat up this lovely lady I met there. Everything appeared to be going well. There was plenty of eye contact and on a couple of occasions she even reached for my face and looked intently into my eyes. I was on to a cracker! She was slurring her words so she was obviously drunk. Maybe she'd lie back and think of Ireland, I thought. Summoning all my charm I asked for her phone number, before staggering off to get a pen and paper. After promising her for ten minutes that, "Of course I'll ring you…" she eventually appeared to give in, and scribbled something on the piece of paper. I sobered up pretty quickly when I unfolded it and read, "How can I ring you – I'm deaf, you GOBSHITE."
DONAL BEHAN, VIA E-MAIL

FELINE FELONY

I'm a graduate in pharmaceutical science, and a couple of years ago spent some time on work experience with the Forensic Science Service. One night I was taken out by two undercover coppers to a stake-out on the outskirts of a farm, where they suspected the owner was babysitting a consignment of drugs. In the small hours of the morning and bored out of our skulls, we saw the farmer come out, sling a black bag into the boot of his car and drive off. We followed him to a local lake, where he dumped the sack and returned to the house. Thinking he'd dropped off a consignment of Class As I readied my testing kit, as one of the cops waded in to retrieve the sack – but when he opened it he found not drugs, but two dead cats and a couple of bricks. So, disgusted by the farmer, and annoyed by the long stakeout, wet and cold, we barrelled it back, crept up to the farmhouse, leant the dead cats against the front door, paws out, pressed the doorbell and legged it. Savage justice!
IAN, VIA E-MAIL

LOVER NOT A FIGHTER

During a night on the town, I managed to pull the most amazing-looking girl and take her home, leaving my friends in the club. After a good half-hour of shagging, my stamina failed me. So I could "re-group" I started to go down on her, but before long my flatmate called my mobile. Apparently a fight had started at the club after I left, and my mate was in hospital. I chucked some clothes on and rushed straight to his bedside and by the time I got to casualty, the police were already there. They promptly arrested me and when I protested my innocence, the policeman wouldn't believe I'd only just got to the hospital and knew nothing of the fight. The police kept telling me to stop lying, as it was obvious from my blood-splattered face what I'd been up to that night. Hmm – maybe I should have kept my eyes open when going down on my lady...
NATHAN THOMAS, WALES

HORSE ON PARADE

My girlfriend has a horse and I accompany her round the country to horse shows, which I find a bit boring. One day she let me sit on her horse and walk with him between events. I must admit I felt quite good up there – especially as I saw quite a few females smiling at me. I was grinning away at everyone until I got off the horse and my girlfriend shouted, "Look!" I peered underneath and there was a two-foot willy hanging down for all to see!

RYAN WEBBER, CHESHIRE

MIND THE DOG

Hoping to earn some brownie points, I decided to do some chores round the house for my wife. It was a glorious afternoon so the doors were thrown open and our pet toy poodle was free to roam. After an hour or so I was hanging up the washing when I saw my neighbour staring over the fence. "Lovely morning for it, Mrs Moody," I beamed, to which she replied, "That's disgusting," and stormed off. I was shocked, so I checked for the offending pair of skid-marked pants, but all was clear. It was then I noticed Dotty the poodle running round the garden with my wife's 12-inch vibrator in its mouth.

MIKE BENNET, MIDLOTHIAN

When Marie stuck her head out to see what was going on, I got a bit cockier and started punting my football higher and higher into the air…

Dribbler lacks attention

Back in the sixth-form my girlfriend, Marie, dumped me for some guy at university. Vowing to win her back, I came up with what I thought was an elaborate scheme to show I was much more of a man than "Mr BA in Turf Management". I played football for the school team, so next Sunday afternoon I showed up outside her house and began dazzling the street's inhabitants with my silky ball control…

GURPAL SINGH, SUTTON COLDFIELD

Eventually I got carried away and lost control of the ball but my reward was a nice beaming smile from Marie, so I scooted off to retrieve it…

The last thing I remember before I woke up in hospital was her scream … and I didn't even get a pity date.

True Stories 2

STUDENT PONG NAILED

I had good reason to feel smug with myself. It had taken me ages to persuade this really classy girl to go out with me and even longer to get her back to my student flat. We were all set to enjoy tea and toast but I felt I had to apologise for our manky toaster that makes everything smell burnt. My helpful guest joked, "I know what you students are like, but have you tried cleaning it?" She pulled out the bottom crumb tray to reveal the charred but very recognisable body of a mouse burnt to the sort of crisp that only being trapped and repeatedly toasted over a number of weeks can achieve. I never saw my dream girl again... and to be honest I haven't been too keen on toast either!

N WILKINS, WEST SUSSEX

BEHOLD THE CLAW!

Studying at Heriot-Watt University in Edinburgh, I used to play in an inter-university indoor football competition. One day I went in for a challenge, resulting in an excruciating pain in my left ankle. Hastily excusing myself from the game I hopped to the nearby sports union reception desk, where I sat waiting for an ice-pack and the likely diagnosis of a broken ankle. All of a sudden I felt sick and vomited everywhere, rapidly going into a state of medical shock. My hands then spasmed into a locked, claw-like position and, shaking, I toppled inelegantly into my puddle of spew on the floor. At this precise moment who should stride in through the doors but the entire Tongan rugby squad – in training for a friendly against Scotland on our pitches – along with a camera crew from Sky Sports, who proceeded to film the entire incident. After seeing the footage my so-called mates started calling me "The Claw" – a nickname that persists to this day, made even worse by the knowledge that in reality my injury amounted to no more than a swollen ankle.

GRAHAM "THE CLAW" MCIVOR, EDINBURGH

Out of the mouths of babes

Watching *Lord Of The Rings* with the family, my 17-year-old sister asked, "When were all the creatures from Middle Earth around? Was it before or after the dinosaurs?"

I recently overheard one of our three secretaries asking, "How many kilos in a kilogram?" What's worse is that the other two didn't know either.

While taking the last of ther three daily inhalers, my girlfriend exclaimed, "I seem to spend half my life just breathing in!"

NURSE! THE SCREEN!

Being a male nurse I get to meet plenty of fit female colleagues and recently pulled a fine filly of a nurse. After spending plenty on wine and flowers I took her back to my place, where we began to undress. She then told me she was untouched by human hands! I was over the moon at having the chance to show this lovely lady my tried-and-tested techniques, and lost no time, expertly stripping her naked as we rolled back and forth across the bed. Just as I was about to inspect her sexy body I noticed a sharp increase in her moaning – followed by a sudden shrieking! She'd only rolled over onto my video's remote control, setting it off and playing back the lesbian porno tape I'd earlier been "sampling". She jumped up and legged it straight out! It's the one and only time I've ever had reason to curse my stash of hot lesbian bongo flicks…

GARY, CHICHESTER

Out of the mouths of babes

My girlfriend Christine was telling her mates about a friend of mine who was on the England karate team, only for one of them to ask, "What song does he sing?"

Arriving at Heathrow, my sister squealed with excitement on seeing the air traffic control tower. "Oooh!" she exclaimed. "I've never seen a lighthouse before!" She's studying law at university.

Sitting round the breakfast table, my sister stared at the bottle of milk before asking how farmers could tell the difference between semi-skimmed and full-cream cows.

GOTH GIRL GETS CARRIED AWAY

One night the lads and I went on the piss at a local rock club, the drinks being cheap as hell. Soon I decided I'd sample a bit of goth for the night. One girl stood out: decent body, clad in PVC with jet black hair, black make-up and those long fake fingernails. So I made my move, got chatting, bought her a few drinks and I was in! We went back to her place and got on with the job. It was great – I could feel her long fingernails going down my back as I worked away, then she grabbed my arse as she reached a climax. Her index finger went straight up my arsehole! I screamed at her to take it out, and as she did the fake fingernail came off in my hole. Every time I moved I could feel the thing digging in, but too embarrassed to go to hospital I asked her to remove it with tweezers. It must have taken the best part of an hour, and for the rest of the weekend I was walking round like I'd just shat myself. No more cheap drinking for me.

DANIEL COLBOURNE, SOMERSET

LEZZA'S HONOUR REMAINS INTACT

A few years ago I was working in London. Ambling through Leicester Square one evening, I became aware that a lesbian couple walking hand-in-hand some yards ahead were receiving a ferocious amount of abuse from a gaggle of beered-up Sunderland fans. I couldn't fathom how the couple had possibly provoked this verbal bombardment – from my vantage point behind them, the only reason I could detect for the jeers and catcalls was that the leggy babe's partner looked to be at least three decades older and had combined a garish snakeskin trouser suit with a streaked blonde quasi-mullet. Eager to demonstrate my sensitive, enlightened side to the lass I was seeing at the time, I commented: "That's awful – have you heard the stick those tossers are giving that lesbian couple, just 'cos one's a bit older than the other?" I must have spoken a little too loudly however, as I was mortified when the aged "lesbian" wheeled around to fix me with a withering stare. It was Peter Stringfellow.

JIM OLDFIELD, MOSBOROUGH

MIDNIGHT PISSER

Last Christmas I stayed with a friend and his family in their country house. Despite the presence of dozens of grandparents and cousins my mate and I still managed to get pole-axed, crawling into bed in the early hours. Some time later I woke up desperate to piss, but on stumbling out of my bedroom I was surrounded by closed doors. Unwilling to walk in on someone, I decided to relieve myself off the bedroom balcony. Imagine my bewilderment when I came down to breakfast next morning to find paramedics carting my mate's grandfather out on a stretcher. Apparently the old codger had stepped out for his morning constitutional and slipped on a patch of ice, screwing his back. Of course, my bedroom was directly above the accident blackspot: my golden shower had frozen and sent the old bird off to two weeks in hospital. A plumber arrived and spent hours searching for the "leak". I admitted nothing, but did put a little salt on my icy discharge.

DAN R, LONDON

Hey mate –
I don't think that
hose is properly
attached…

Music lover
gets a coating

A few years ago I was at a well-known Scottish music festival when my missus decided she needed the toilet. This being Day Two, and her being a proper lady, she was freaked out by the condition of the crappers: tampons, poo, piss – you know the drill. So she was excited to spot a row of Portaloos that were being cleaned, and dragged me over to the hopefully now spotless bogs…

**GARETH MCWALTER,
DUNDEE**

No sooner had she closed the door…

Ker-spludge!!

Me, I just took another swig of vodka and enjoyed the rest of the weekend.

True Stories 2

Out of the mouths of babes

My mother-in-law was struggling with a celebrity crossword. "It's Sam somebody…" she said. I reeled off all the Sams I knew, to no avail. Then she said, "I've got it! Sam Anthamumba!"

In the pub, I asked my girlfriend's friend if she could tell me the cricket score, as my view of the TV was obscured. "Seventeen-nil!" she proudly exclaimed.

Organising the Royal Naval Air Station Yeovilton International Air Day, I took a phone call from a lady asking if it was to be an indoor event. The Red Arrows were due to appear!

SAUNA TREASURE

In order to support myself at university, I used to work as an instructor at a private health gym. One morning while inspecting the saunas before we opened, I made an interesting find: a ten-inch gold vibrator! Carefully sheathing my hand in a carrier bag I took hold of the buzzing beauty, before placing it in the lost property box. Later that day my manager asked me to bring the item to his office for closer inspection. He plunged his hand straight into the bag, took out the tool and waved it in front of the by-now packed office, as the discovery had been the sole object of conversation among the staff all day. A jolly chap, he pointed it at each of the female employees in turn, saying, "Which of you girls left this, then?" before putting the vibe up to his nose and sniffing from one end to the other. "I recognise that smell – is it you, Julie?" he continued. You can imagine the look on his face when, in a stage whisper, I had to inform him that I'd actually found it in the men's sauna.
TW, BARNSLEY

CARPET MYSTERY SOLVED

Having a reputation as a Mr Fix-It and being the kind-hearted bloke that I am, I agreed to pop round and tune in my elderly next-door neighbour's newly-acquired VCR. While I was lying on my front connecting the necessary cables and tuning to the correct channels using the remote control, I couldn't help but notice the random orangey-brown streaking pattern in the old gimmer's blue carpet, just inches from my nose. It soon became clear what the pattern was when the old boy's poodle came into the room: it was dragging itself along the carpet by its front legs in a sat-upright kind of position, its hind legs and feet pointing to the ceiling. Whether this was a novel way of wiping its arse or it had a bad case of worms, I didn't wait to find out – I was far too busy legging it to the dry cleaners.

SIMON HARLEY, LANCASHIRE

LUNCHTIME GOBBLE TURNS SOUR

We were having a new bathroom installed, so I decided to work from home for a couple of days to deal with any problems that might arise. However, bored and with unsupervised access to the internet, I soon started surfing for porn instead – resulting in a phone call to my girlfriend asking her to drop in during her lunch hour. As the builders munched their sandwiches we snuck off to the bedroom, where my young lady gave me an awesome blow-job. Mission complete, I happily headed off to clean myself up – not knowing the bathroom floorboards had been ripped out. I duly went crashing through the kitchen ceiling and ended up hanging on to a supporting joist – ensuring that my flaccid, lipstick-covered member was flopping around in plain view of the builders making themselves a pot of tea.

PJ, VIA E-MAIL

SLOW-BURN PRANK COMES OFF

About a year after graduating from uni, I had a bunch of mates round for the evening, including my on/off girlfriend. As the night wore on I managed to entice her down to the garage for a ciggie and a bit of a flirt, in the hope of her becoming more "on" than "off". There in the corner I saw my trusty old acoustic guitar, which had been gathering dust since my student days. What could be more effective in wooing my good lady than a few chords? But after a quick strum we noticed a rattling noise coming from inside the hollow-bodied instrument. My ladyfriend reached inside, got a grip on a wad of paper and managed to pull it out. A huge wave of panic suddenly hit me, and I was transported back to my student house-sharing days in Birmingham. Like any group of lads living together, we were prone to springing the odd prank, the longest-running being stashing a particularly depraved item of gay porn in each others' rooms, hoping to catch the unfortunate victim out when a ladyfriend ever happened to stay over. And there, 12 months later, was my soon-to-be-ex-girlfriend clutching a well-thumbed copy of Sex Pigs. It was, without doubt, the best – and slowest – stitch-up any of us ever pulled off.
CHRIS, MACCLESFIELD

HOUND'S SURPRISE

The other day I went with a friend to walk his four dogs in the New Forest. One of the hyperactive pups came running up to me with a lovely stick, so, being a dog-friendly person, I patted him on the head, then tugged it out of his mouth. At this point, the lovely lab kept launching himself at me before I could throw it for him to fetch. Insisting on good manners, I had a short battle with said dog, yelling, "Sit!" to him. Eventually, I got him to comply, at which point my friend looked over and asked what the hell I had in my hand? I looked at the "stick", which turned out to be a lovely deer leg, complete with hoof. I dropped it like lightning, shrieking swearwords whilst my doggy friend retrieved it with that lovely labrador smile.
BECCA HALLEWELL, DORSET

THAT'S NOT GRAVY!

Last summer, I was cooking a Sunday roast to impress this hot girl I worked with. Slaving away in the kitchen for an hour before she arrived, I was repeatedly interrupted by the snotty-nosed neighbourhood kids kicking their football into my back garden from the adjoining playing field. After retrieving the ball for about the fifth or sixth time I decided to put a stop to it – told them to, "Fuck off!" and kept their ball. Pretty soon my lady arrived and, realising she'd forgotten to bring any wine,

Out of the mouths of babes

During a dispute with my mate about who was taller, my girlfriend made us stand back-to-back. When she declared that my mate was taller, I protested. "Come and have a look for yourself," she told me, calmly.

Watching that great British zombie flick 28 Days Later, my beautiful young lady got agitated at the point in the film where we see a wind farm. "If there ain't any electricity," she piped up, "how come those wind turbines are going around?"

offered to go to the local shop and pick some up. As the cooking was doing alright by itself, I went with her. We returned a few minutes later but now the smell coming from the cooker was so putrid we started retching. The local kids had let themselves in, taken their ball back, crapped in my boiled veg, and then returned the pan to the boil. The little swines.

RK, VIA E-MAIL

FHM
LADIES'
CONFESSIONS

Fantasist goes too far

Several years ago (when I was young and unwise about the ways of the world), I had this rather naughty "habit" of getting kicks from secretly masturbating in front of people. On several occasions I sat opposite strangers on a train, casually placed my coat over my lap and ever so subtly brought myself off without ever alerting the poor passengers sitting opposite me. Clearly this became a bit of a challenge to myself and I would find myself in ever more dodgy situations. Eventually I realised it had got a bit too silly when I managed to come in the back seat of a car sitting in between two church youth group leaders on the way to a church picnic...

KATINKA, LONDON

EXPERIMENT GOES WRONG

I met this really fit guy in a bar and because I hadn't had sex for a while was very horny and feeling quite experimental. Once we got back to his place foreplay was short and we went straight to some very hard shagging. A little later I thought things were getting a bit tedious and I'd better spice things up. So I slid my hand around to his arse and slipped a couple of fingers inside him. He wasn't shocked at all and we carried on with our rude fun. A bit later we moved on to slower canoodling. Shortly he took my fingers and licked them one by one. However, once he got to my index finger he started to gag and then threw up all over my naked body. It's the worst night I've ever had and I've since given up alcohol.

RACHEL, VIA E-MAIL

PUB SESSION LEAVES EVIDENCE

My husband and I used to run a pub. One night after closing we decided to get down and dirty all round the bar. On our way around the rooms we left a trail of discarded clothes, and after a full-on session went to bed. The next morning I went down to open up and at the bottom of the stairs found a neatly piled set of clothes and a pair of shoes. Tucked inside the shoes were a pair of knickers and a bra, the cleaner having done a little extra tidying! She just smiled and said good morning and the incident was never mentioned. Of course, I couldn't look her in the eye for a week.

ZOE, TAMWORTH

ONE-NIGHTER GOES PEAR-SHAPED

After having a few too many at my local one night I ended up staggering back to this guy's house. We stumbled up the stairs in the dark, both feeling really horny. After a bit of fumbling around on the bed he finally got started. He'd only been pumping away for a few seconds when I felt a warm, wet substance shooting up inside me. At first I thought that maybe he'd come really quickly but then to my horror I realised that it wasn't his ejaculation he couldn't control, but his bladder. I'll never forget the embarrassed look on his face.

EMMA, VIA E-MAIL

CLUBBER GETS SURPRISE

On the way to a nightclub in Manchester with my mate, I simply couldn't wait to go for a piss, so I decided I'd have to go in a market stall which was in the middle of the street. Thinking I was alone, I dropped my knickers to piss on this pile of cardboard inside the stall. But as I crouched down and began to release my wee

I suddenly realised I was pissing on a tramp underneath all the boxes. I nearly died of shock and pulled up my knickers without finishing.
ANON, VIA E-MAIL

HUNGOVER LADY FORGETS TO DOUCHE

After getting drunk with a group of friends on a hen night, I got talking to this fit bloke and went back to his for some really great sex. Then I duly left, not wanting the awkward morning-after goodbyes. The following night I had a date with a guy I had just started seeing. Feeling all hungover we just decided to get a video out. Later that night we were getting horny and he decided to put his fingers up my lady flower. Imagine my embarrassment when he pulled out a condom with spunk still in it. It must have slipped off during my sex session the night before! We never went out much after that.
CATHERINE, VIA E-MAIL

RANDY DAUGHTER SPOTTED

Years ago when I still lived at home I woke up one morning feeling very horny and decided to have a fiddle under the covers. God knows how long later, but after one fantastic orgasm, I opened my eyes to find my bedroom door ajar. I was horrified as I always slept with it closed and it could only mean one thing – my dad had looked in on me as he occasionally would. The thought of him seeing my hand working furiously under the covers was so shameful that I tried to keep out of his way all day. That night as I was off to bed he said, "Good night – and behave yourself!"
DANI, BOURNEMOUTH

LEZZER REVEALS TRUTH

At our university there's a girl all the lads love. On Valentine's Day she received something like 40 or so cards, to my pitiful none. She taunts them all the time, dances on the tables, shows her ass and flashes her tits at them. Pity for them that she's a lezzer who's going out with me! And we have a great plan to eat each other out on the coffee table in the conference room.
ANON, VIA E-MAIL

MASSAGE DOES TRICK

A few years ago my boyfriend surprised me with a holiday to Turkey to mark our anniversary. One day while he was sunbathing at our hotel I decided to go for a massage in the spa, hoping to relax after virtually a whole week of never leaving our hotel room. I settled down on the table and closed my eyes while the masseuse worked her magic. So relaxed was I after 15 minutes of therapeutic rubbing that I didn't flinch when I felt something touch my privates. I opened my legs a bit further and my generous masseuse kept on fingering me, until I had a

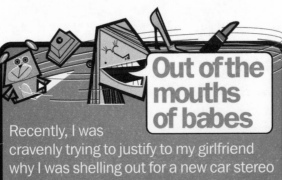

Out of the mouths of babes

Recently, I was cravenly trying to justify to my girlfriend why I was shelling out for a new car stereo system. I told her it featured a television, satellite navigation and a DVD player. "Cool," she replied. "It sounds like the bee's bollocks."

On holiday recently in Mexico, we got chatting to a couple in the bar and discovered they were from Austria. "Oh wow," said my girlfriend. "Do you speak Ostrich?"

On a recent trip to the beach my now ex-girlfriend noticed a sign that read, "ALL REFUSE TO BE PUT IN BIN." "That's a stupid sign," she said, puzzled. "Who would agree to be put in a bin?"

My female housemate recently tried to solve a query that had clearly been bothering her for some time. "You know nipples?" she asked, puzzled. "What are they called on men?" This from a woman allegedly studying law!

Ladies' Confessions

Out of the mouths of babes

While having a conversation with my mum, the talk turned to homosexuality. "I could never be gay," she said. "I just couldn't have one of them things shoved up my arse."

My mate was telling his girlfriend about an acquaintance who'd been badly beaten up, and as a result had staples in his head. "Christ," she exclaimed, obviously shocked. "Why would anyone attack someone with a stapler?"

great orgasm. Now when my husband asks me to talk dirty I know exactly which "fantasy" to tell him about.

SHELLEY, WREXHAM

WRONG CREAM DAUBED

When I shared a house at university I woke up one morning with a bit of an itch around my bits. In my still-groggy state I figured it must be thrush, so I took some cream from my bedside locker and applied it. Pretty soon I realised all was not well as the sensation had turned from a slight itch to a burning pain that made me cry out loud. That's when I took a second look at the cream – it wasn't Canestan as I'd thought, but a tube of Deep Heat left by my ex. My screams woke my housemates who found me squatting in the bath dousing myself with cold water. But it wasn't sympathy all round, because in my dash to the bathroom I'd left my bedroom door open, leaving my housemates to see our married landlord in my bed.

EMMA, VIA E-MAIL

NUMBER CALLED IN HASTE

One morning I got up feeling a tad horny so I thought it'd be a good idea to ring my man on his mobile and give him some action down the line. I got myself positioned, phone in one hand and hot pie in the other. The second the phone answered I went straight into it, proceeding to tell him how I was getting very horny, lying in bed working myself off and imagining that I had another girl naked beside me. Suddenly a voice interrupted me just when I was really starting to enjoy myself. Oh shit – it wasn't Al's voice, it was his dad's. In all the excitement, instead of pressing "Al" on the mobile I had pressed "Al Snr". I didn't wait to hear what he had to say, and up to now he hasn't mentioned it, although now when we call round he seems much friendlier than before...

DI, VIA E-MAIL

DJ GETS CAUGHT

On a night out in Blackpool when I was 18, I got speaking to a DJ in a club. After the club (and several Aftershocks) I was unable to walk properly, so the DJ I had been chatting with offered to help. Of course he ended up taking me to his house and telling me it was okay to spend the night. After much kissing and groping, he got his manhood out and asked for a blow-job. Being off my head I happily agreed, despite wearing a brace on the top row of my teeth. After about 10 minutes I got bored but when I went to pull away, a small piece of loose wire on my brace pierced through his foreskin and he grabbed my head in shock. We were stuck because he was too scared to yank my head away quickly. In the end he got on his mobile to his ex-girlfriend to come round and help. When she came in she burst out laughing, pulled out her camera, took a few pictures and left. I was so embarrassed that I pulled away quickly and tore a strip out of his foreskin.

EMMA, VIA E-MAIL

TOURISTS LEAVE SOUVENIR

Early this year my boyfriend and I went to Fort William in Scotland for a cosy weekend. After taking a cable car, we did some exploring and stumbled across the remains of Inverlochy Castle. My boyfriend started getting all horny, so I pulled up my skirt and bent over so he could take me from behind. After ten minutes or so he came over my bum, then wiped me clean with my panties, which we left there as a souvenir. Only after we emerged from our hideaway did we notice an old woman walking her dog. The old dear paused a moment, looked down and then muttered something about having no respect for a 700-year-old castle.

AMANDA, RUNCORN

KEBABERIE GETS STEAMY

One day, after an afternoon spent drinking, my boyfriend and I decided to visit our local kebab shop. The man serving us always stares at my 36D breasts, and as it was summer I went in there in a see-through top and pink bra. We ordered two chicken kebabs, and the guy serving said to me in a sexual manner, "Would you like some extra chilli sauce?" "Yes, please," I replied, "and may I use your toilet?" So I went off to the loo, shortly followed by my boyfriend. When I had my knickers round my ankles he began rogering me from behind, when suddenly Mr Kebab turned up with his knob out. My boyfriend said to him, "Do you want to feel her fanny?" which he did and started wanking. In two seconds flat he shot his load all over the floor and ran back to his duties. After my boyfriend finished me off, we went back in to collect our nosh. He charged us full price for two kebabs, but we got home to find only one! We felt so stitched up we haven't been back since.

LINDA, KENT

BOSS ENJOYS MORNING RELIEF

While at work on a dull Monday morning I began to feel horny, so I went into my boss's office (who I'd been seeing for two months), got under the desk and started sucking him off. It was one of the best blow-jobs I'd ever given. Then suddenly the door opened. The MD came in and said, "We're waiting for you." To which he replied, "I'm coming," seconds later spraying his load down my throat. He'd forgotten about the board meeting he was supposed to be in. For the rest of the day we couldn't stop grinning at each other.

PENNY, EAST SUSSEX

Teens get nude treat

Me and my boyfriend went for a go on the haunted house ride at Alton Towers. We sat in our cart all alone, he looked at me and I looked at him and in seconds we were shagging semi-nude in the cart. It was the best sex ever but then there was a flash. We both stopped, quickly got dressed and pretended nothing happened. We got off the ride and were going to walk past the photo stall casually. On the way past we had a quick glance and there I was, tits out on number 355. We walked straight past but a few seconds later I heard a voice from behind shout, "I'll have two of 355 please!" We looked around and shouting at the lady behind the counter were about eight 15-year-olds all asking for photo 355.
STEFF, VIA E-MAIL

SCARF COVERS NAUGHTINESS

My scroogy ex-boyfriend was so unbelievably tight-fisted, he never once paid for me to go to the pictures. So to get back at him I decided to snog someone behind his back, who, unfortunately, covered my neck in loads of nasty lovebites. The next morning I had to wear a scarf to cover the bites. My ex complimented the stylish scarf and to this day doesn't know the real reason why I wore it.
HELEN, VIA E-MAIL

Ladies' Confessions

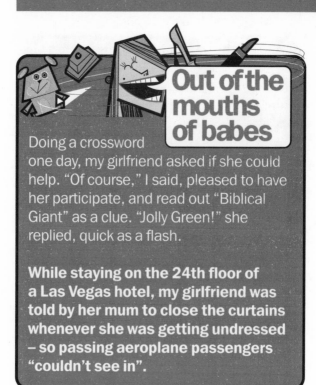

Out of the mouths of babes

Doing a crossword one day, my girlfriend asked if she could help. "Of course," I said, pleased to have her participate, and read out "Biblical Giant" as a clue. "Jolly Green!" she replied, quick as a flash.

While staying on the 24th floor of a Las Vegas hotel, my girlfriend was told by her mum to close the curtains whenever she was getting undressed – so passing aeroplane passengers "couldn't see in".

HORNY LADY IMPROVISES

I was in my final year at uni and having been working hard for my exams, the days I got to spend with my boyfriend were few and far between. One morning, feeling horny, I went to the bathroom to get ready. As I was doing the normal routine I saw that one of my flatmates had invested in an electric toothbrush.
I perched on the edge of the bath and while my other housemates thought I was cleaning my teeth I was having the time of my life with this new vibrating brush. To this day the owner still doesn't know what I got up to – the only person who does is my boyfriend, who can never look at the toothbrush in the same way.
SP, BRIGHTON

HOLIDAYMAKER IMPROVISES TWICE

Last summer in Ibiza I was sooo wild. One night I had a steamy session with a guy I'd picked up in a bar. Afterwards, I needed a cool midnight dip, but he headed to a club – charming! Still, I was determined to go skinny-dipping. Just one problem; nothing to tie my hair back with, so I picked up one of the condoms we'd used, rinsed it out and used it to tie my hair in a ponytail. I wasn't alone for long. A good-looking local lad was swimming nearby and to cut a long story

short, a look turned into a snog, a snog turned into a grope, and pretty soon I was back on heat. We dried off but now I had another problem: no condoms. Then I had an idea. I told him I was going for a pee in the bushes and not to look. It was a bit fiddly, but I finally undid the condom from my hair, went back to my Latin lover, pulled it over his cock and used it to shag him senseless! Just doing my bit for recycling.
"B", WORCESTER

JACK THE LAD CAUSES PANIC

A few years ago, I fancied this lad who goes with anything with a pulse, so inevitably ended up in the sack with him. Our session culminated with him requesting to shoot his load on my tits. Obligingly I lay back and closed my eyes while he started masturbating and sure enough, I soon felt a hot runny liquid on my chest. To make him think I was enjoying it I started rubbing my hands all over my breasts and belly. That was until I opened my eyes and saw my chest covered with blood, as well as the palms of my hands. He hadn't actually come yet and was still wanking, with this blood pumping out his cock! "It's all right," he said. "I shagged this lass a few months ago and she was a bit dry and this has happened ever since." Well needless to say I was no longer in the mood, so I made my excuses and left. See ya, scummer!
JO, VIA E-MAIL

FEUDING FLATMATES SHARE MORE THAN JUST A LOVER

A few years ago I flat-shared with a real bitch. She would snare blokes, keep them on for a couple of weeks then dump them. She "joked" that I should have her cast-offs as I hadn't had a boyfriend for months. Anyway, one Saturday morning I awoke to find that she'd left a note saying she wouldn't be back until Sunday night and that if John (her current lover) called, to tell him that she'd left for good. She had only been seeing him for a week and even by her standards that was quick. An hour later John knocked at the door. He looked really upset when I told him she had gone so I invited him in. Then I did what any woman would do under those circumstances and decided to make him feel better by shagging him, which was fantastic. Best of all we did it on the bitch's bed. When she returned I feigned concern and badgered her about John and why she'd dumped him. Eventually she just blew up. "If you must know," she screamed, "I found out that I had gonorrhoea and I couldn't face telling him." So my revenge was short-lived: turns out she had given it to him, and he'd given it to me. Moral: always wear a condom.

HELEN, VIA E-MAIL

HORNY STUDENT SAVOURS SLOPPY SECONDS

Feeling really randy at uni not long ago, I drunkenly ended up with one of the sexy footballers from the university team. Back at mine, we had a pretty rampant session and were just finishing off when I got a call from my ex-boyfriend, a complete tosser who lived above me. Because he was in such an emotional

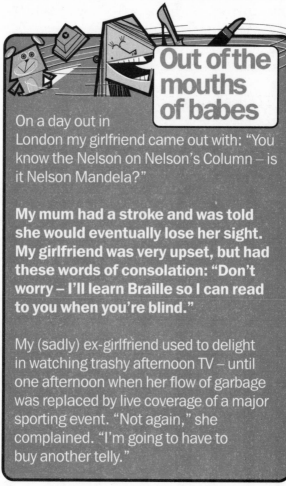

Out of the mouths of babes

On a day out in London my girlfriend came out with: "You know the Nelson on Nelson's Column – is it Nelson Mandela?"

My mum had a stroke and was told she would eventually lose her sight. My girlfriend was very upset, but had these words of consolation: "Don't worry – I'll learn Braille so I can read to you when you're blind."

My (sadly) ex-girlfriend used to delight in watching trashy afternoon TV – until one afternoon when her flow of garbage was replaced by live coverage of a major sporting event. "Not again," she complained. "I'm going to have to buy another telly."

state, I agreed to go up and see him, telling the sexy footballer that I'd be back shortly, but neglecting to mention that it was my ex-boyfriend I was visiting. So, having heard my ex's sob story of what a bad night he'd had, I ended up shagging him, too. You can only imagine the pleasure it gave me knowing that not only had he got sloppy seconds, but that he'd got his mate's man juices all over his cock. All in all, a productive evening.
LUCY, ESSEX

PAIR GET SACRILEGIOUS

My boyfriend and I hired a church for a party we were due to be having. Not wanting to stay at my mum's house and with no money for a bed and breakfast prior to the bash, my boyfriend suggested we stay in the church as we had already been given the keys. So we bought beer and sat in the aisles. Everything started out very romantically – the church had nice spotlights shining on the altar. But not long later I found myself, legs spread and dress hitched up, being joyfully screwed across an altar. What a sinful night that was!
VICKY, BRADFORD

LEZZER FOOLS MUM

My mum doesn't realise I'm a lesbian, and she'd go mad if she found out. A year after meeting my first girlfriend, we're still going strong, though there was almost trouble one night, when after giving her a good licking-out and returning home, my mum said she could smell fish on my breath. I made the excuse that I'd had cod for tea. Close one!
LAURA, NORTHANTS

RANDY BLOKE GETS SHOT IN THE EYE

My boyfriend always had a thing about wanting to come on my tits, and one evening, after a seriously heavy night on the town, I finally gave in to his wish. I lay on the bed tossing him off while he sat over me. Just as he was about to come, he looked down at his proud manhood to get the full view, only to receive a hot wad of his own love wee in his eye!
JO, VIA E-MAIL

LUSH LEAVES MARK

A few years ago I was in my local celebrating my 20th birthday, getting absolutely wrecked. I somehow got home and really needed to be sick. I made it to the bathroom and stuck my head down the pan, but then the urge to shit came over me. There was nothing I could do but shit in the position I was in. Wearing only a G-string, and with the poo being of a semi-solid consistency, you can imagine what happened. I left the bathroom with what could only be described as a cow-pat on the new bathroom carpet.

LESLEY, STIRLING

FOODIE FILLS UP

While living at my parents' house, my boyfriend and I regularly ordered Chinese takeaways. We then locked ourselves in my room and ate it away from the prying eyes of my sister. One evening, though, I'd been reading tips on how to give an extra-special blow-job, so I was keen to try out my new tips on my man. We soon got

Out of the mouths of babes

My wife rang me at work to tell me her car had a flat tyre. "But I don't think it's too bad," she said. "It's only flat at the bottom."

After watching Japan v Belgium, my friend turned over to the next match on a different channel, which kicked off ten minutes later. "That's amazing!" his girlfriend said. "How did they get the fans from the last game out and the new fans in so fast?"

On the piss late one night in Prague, I needed to find a hole in the wall. "But where are you going to get the money changed this late at night?" pointed out my beloved.

Drunkard pays off fare

While I was a skint student I worked part-time in a restaurant where the owners held a Christmas party for all the staff at the local nightclub. Towards the end of the night I still hadn't pulled and was so pissed I was finding it hard to stand. I decided to leave and went outside to catch a cab. On the way home the cab driver and I started to talk and before I knew it we were outside my house. One thing led to another and I ended up giving him a blow-job: when he came I spat it out. The worst part was I was so drunk I then rummaged in my bag, pulled out a tenner, paid him and left. To this day my friends still take the piss that I paid a man £10 to give him a blow-job.

REN, NOTTINGHAM

down to business, making lots of amorous noises and slurps. I was just getting him there when my sister knocked at the door and asked, "What are you eating?" Little did she know I had a mouthful of dick!

AMANDA, LIVERPOOL

BOSS GOES EVERYWHERE

Managing to attract my gorgeous-but-married boss, we took to shagging at every opportunity. While working one dull Saturday, he came into

the office unexpectedly, desperate for some of my personal skills, so we nipped off to the loo. Time was precious so – with trousers round ankles and thong round bum-cheeks – we went at it, him behind as I hung on to the door handles. As he was about to come, I jumped off and whipped around in an attempt to catch his juice in my mouth. Alas, I mistimed and ended up covered in the stuff! Hastily cleaning up, I returned to the office. It was only at the end of the day that my workmates told me that my hair was covered in sticky jizz – the humiliation!
JANE, VIA E-MAIL

Out of the mouths of babes

Discussing the Incredible Hulk TV series one lunchtime, we established that Dr David Banner was played by Bill Bixby and the Hulk by Lou Ferrigno. The office blonde chipped in, "Was it two different actors then?"

COPS GET EYEFUL

After a night out clubbing, me and my fella headed home. On the way back, however, things got horny and we ended up having sex on a traffic island surrounded by bushes. They concealed us, or so we thought. Mid-shag, I looked up to see a copper peering over the bushes! I got up, covered in mud, thinking this was the worst moment ever. But it got worse, as there by the side of the road was not one cop but a whole van of them. I could hear their cheers as we scurried off down the road, shame-faced.
VICKI, MIDDLESBROUGH

BRIDE ENJOYS LESBIAN PRE-NUPS

The night before my friend's wedding, the bride-to-be decided to handcuff herself to me for the rest of the night. While in the toilet of a nightclub, she told me how sexy I was and started to kiss and fondle me. Fuelled by alcohol, I didn't stop her and soon we were on the floor, fingers and tongues everywhere until I had the best orgasm ever. The next day, sitting in the church, I couldn't help but smile at her new husband, knowing that just 12 hours earlier I had my tongue between his lovely wife's legs.

N, VIA E-MAIL

LOVERS DAMAGE PRIDE AND JOY

Every Christmas back home in Australia, I travel down south with my boyfriend's family to stay in their beach house. Last Christmas my boyfriend and I were desperate for some time alone so we took off in his dad's utility truck. We found a nice spot in the middle of the bush where we knew we were completely alone. We climbed onto the back of the truck and my boyfriend stood on the tray while I sat on the roof of the car with my legs wrapped around his waist. We had the most amazing shag and were getting quite rough with one another. When we arrived back at the beach house the whole family were sitting on the balcony. My boyfriend's father (who loves his truck), jumped out of his seat and stared at the roof of the car. Not only did he discover that my arse and hands had made perfect indents in the roof, but also that I had left my semen-soggy panties in the tray at the back. After that it was a very awkward Christmas dinner!

SARAH, VIA E-MAIL

SKINNYDIPPING LEADS TO BRA JIGGERY

On a boozy night out me and my mates met some really hot blokes and went back to their hotel, where we all went swimming – naked. After some time, we decided to go back to their rooms to continue the fun so went to get dressed. I could hear sniggering and one of the blokes held up a bra with padded tissues stuffed down it. They joked about whose it could be. My friends all retrieved their bras and I picked one up too, and we all said it definitely wasn't ours! Off we went to their rooms for some

Ladies' Confessions

Out of the mouths of babes

On a night flight back from Florida, my wife looked out of the window at the featureless sky and said, "Are we flying above the stars?" D'oh!

Walking past a building site, I mused out loud as to how such large cranes were built. My always-helpful girlfriend chipped in with, "If I was building one of those I'd start at the top and work down." Genius.

Me and a few workmates were coming out with various crap double entendres. Listening in, a female colleague blurted out: "I don't know what double entendres are – will one of you fill me in?"

Watching George Foreman flogging his "lean, mean, grilling machine" on TV, my girlfriend chipped in with: "What does he know about cooking? He plays the banjo."

During a visit to Chessington World Of Adventures with my girlfriend, we found ourselves watching a lion. I jokingly mentioned that it looked like the roaring one at the beginning of MGM films. "That's the most famous lion in the world," replied my girlfriend. "Except for Tony the Tiger, of course."

Watching dolphins in Singapore last year, my girlfriend was mightily impressed by their ability to perform complex tricks. "Well, they are the second most intelligent creatures on Earth," I replied, sagely. "What's the first?" she said, then pondered the answer for a moment: "the dog?" It appears so.

jiggery. But I never did admit that the bra was mine – and to the poor lady whose bra I pinched I'm very sorry, but I just couldn't lose face in front of everyone!
JENNA, LIVERPOOL

HORNY TEMP CAUGHT AT IT

I used to work as a temp a few years back and ended up being posted to a firm of solicitors for a week. On my second day I was feeling really horny and thought no-one would notice if I slipped off to the toilet for five minutes. So I got to the loo, took off my skirt and panties and went for it. Just at the point of climax the toilet door burst open and stood in front of me was my manageress. In my hurry to relieve myself I'd forgotten to lock the door! I was so embarrassed I left the same day.
KELLY, EXETER

SLEEPING HUBBY GETS SHOWER

My husband has this annoying habit after visiting the loo in the middle of the night. He returns to bed, starkers, snuggles up to me to warm up, and then I feel a small trickle of piss down my thigh. I figured revenge was in order so one night I crept to the loo and purposefully didn't wipe myself. I then proceeded to crouch over his sleeping face and shake myself dry. On feeling the urine trickle onto his face, my husband, still fast asleep, stuck out his tongue and lapped up the wee.
DM, HOVE

COUPLE GIVE SHOW

When I was younger I had this fantasy about having sex with other people watching. So one drunken night me and my boyfriend got naked, opened the curtains and with the lights on really went for it. Cue instant abandonment as we spotted a small child opposite watching.
MJ, GREENWICH

DULLARD'S GIRL DOES DIRTY IN FRONT OF HIM

I was going out with this guy for about a year, and to be honest he was not the most exciting of men. One day we decided to spend the day in

Masseur improvises with dildo

I met a lovely masseur who promised me a special treatment. When he arrived at my house, I used my housemate's room, as mine was less than fragrant. Lying on the bed, he massaged me with nice oils but I was more thrilled when I felt a vibration. In his hand was a huge rubbery vibrator, which he worked in and out of my pussy. "Wow, he was well prepared," I thought. He left and I went back to my room. When my housemate came home she stormed in, holding the vibrator in her hand. "You bitch," she hissed. "I've told you to leave my things alone!" Massage man later told me he'd found it under "my" pillow, and put it back there afterwards. Whoops!

ZOE, HANTS

together and I thought this would be the ideal opportunity to spice up our sex life. How wrong I was. Within minutes of arriving at his house he started working on his computer, plus his mate Nick was there. So much for us being alone. But Nick was cute and we got on like a house on fire. We got on so well that when he came into my boyfriend's (freezing) room and got under the duvet, my fella didn't even bat an eyelid. That's when the fun began. My man didn't even notice my quiet little moans caused by his best friend flicking my bean under the duvet! At one point my bloke did turn round but only to see me pretending to be asleep, while the truth was his mate was giving me a fantastic rogering in the spoon position!

KATHRYN, NOTTS

MUM IMPROVISES FOR ODD-JOB MAN

A few years ago we had a visit from a bloke at our local furniture store to fix a broken chest of drawers. I asked him if he would like a drink and he said he'd love a cup of tea. Unfortunately when I opened the fridge, I found we had no milk except, innocently sitting there, a bottle of my recently expressed breast milk ready for my new-born son. There was only one thing for it... I gave him his drink and he chucked it down quick as a flash. He then told me it was the best cup of tea he'd had all day! When I see him in the local furniture store I always have to smile.

LP, BURTON ON TRENT

COUPLE MAKE GOOD USE OF HUSSY

A couple of years ago my fella and I lived above a right man-eater – every weekend we'd hear her at it with a different fella. Secretly this used to be a bit of a turn-on and I'd often end up jumping my man to the sexy sounds. One evening, after we'd indulged in a Saturday afternoon's drinking I saw our neighbour getting a pizza delivered. Figuring that was her in for the night and feeling a bit outrageous thanks to the booze, I bet my man he couldn't get into her knickers. Half an hour later, and

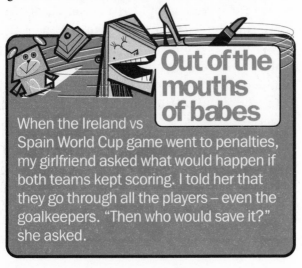

Out of the mouths of babes

When the Ireland vs Spain World Cup game went to penalties, my girlfriend asked what would happen if both teams kept scoring. I told her that they go through all the players – even the goalkeepers. "Then who would save it?" she asked.

after feeding her a bullshit story about going out
for some wine and locking himself out, I was
lying in bed frigging myself off while listening
to my man give her the screwing of her life.
Pretty soon after – and all that night – I was on
the receiving end, too.

RK, VIA E-MAIL

LADY TAKES CHANCE

Weeks ago at work a very cute chap, who I knew
fancied me, asked me out for a drink. He always
seemed lost and lonely, so I thought, why not?
We met at a bar and he was actually very
amusing, so we soon began meeting regularly.
What I noticed was how often he complimented
me on my make-up, and always asked where I'd
bought a particular outfit. One evening he
asked if I'd like to go to his flat for dinner the
next Saturday and I accepted. When the day
came I made sure I looked pretty hot. But when
the door opened at Charles's flat, I was greeted
by a stunning girl. It was only when she said,
"Hello Rosemary," that I realised that it was in
fact Charles! All our meetings suddenly made
sense! For a moment I thought of leaving but
decided to stay and was glad I did. We had a
great evening – "Camilla" cooked us a perfect
meal and of course there was very interesting
conversation. And then at the end of the night,
having sex with a beautiful transvestite was an
amazing experience!

ROSEMARY, VIA E-MAIL

SEX EXPERIMENT GETS TRICKY

After a boozy session my boyfriend and I got
frisky and decided to put objects inside my
pussy. After a cucumber and a wine bottle we
grabbed a marble egg off my mum's
mantelpiece. Imagine my horror when my
fanny sucked it up! After much pleasurable
fingering we had to get a spoon to scoop it out –
the ultimate egg and spoon race…

TOP BIRD, BRUM

SPORTSMAN SEEKS MEMORIES

In my first year at university I had been chasing
the captain of the football team for weeks when
finally (and under the influence of lots of

booze), he showed an interest in me. Not long later we were back at my place shagging as if our lives depended on it. After a few hours the alcohol was wearing off and my juices were drying up, but this guy was absolutely insatiable. Eventually I went fairly numb down below. But then all of a sudden I yelped in pain and shouted, "What the hell are you doing?" It turned out that this bloke had a very strange sexual deviancy – it seems that he got off on shoving his watch up my fanny. His reasoning for this timepiece intrusion was "so that I can smell this and think of you". Needless to say, I didn't go back for more!

P, BERKSHIRE

Out of the mouths of babes

Overhearing a discussion about the supermarket chain Iceland changing its name to The Big Food Group, our female admin clerk at work commented, "That's a strange name for a country."

Chilling at my mate's house, one of his sister's friends asked to see the new conservatory. On viewing she exclaimed, "Wow! It's like a whole different room!"

MUM SOOTHES ROW

During a blazing row my daughter walked out and left her boyfriend at our house. She later called to say that they'd split up but he could sleep over as planned in her room, while she stayed over at her friend's. So he went to buy some beer, returned to her room and watched telly all night. I popped in about midnight as the TV was still on and to my surprise he was spread across the bed asleep and naked, sporting a large erection. Being a single mum and my sex life somewhat on the slow side, temptation got the

better of me and I slowly leaned over the bed and began to suck him off. After a while he began to stir so I grabbed a scarf and wrapped it around his head, saying, "Sorry I was angry," (pretending to be my daughter). I then straddled him, making sure that I pleasured myself good and proper. The next morning, I overheard my daughter and the boyfriend talking about how real an erotic dream felt last night. It got worse when later on she apologised for all the rowing the night before and said she'd decided to stay with him after all. Oops.
CLAIRE, LONDON

SWIMMER GIVES AN EYEFUL

Recently I went to stay at my rich boyfriend's house. I'd been keeping myself trim for him all summer by swimming each morning, so when his dad told me about the pool at the end of the garden I was gutted that I'd left my bikini at home. I didn't catch exactly what he said next, something like, "...no-one's around, so don't worry." The next morning I went down to the pool, bright and early, left my kit by the pool-side and did 20 lengths, *au naturel*. But after my exercise came two horrific shocks. The first was discovering a row of his sisters' spare swimmers in the pool house – obviously his dad meant they weren't around, and I was not to worry about borrowing them! The second shock came when I learnt that the old man next door had been pruning his prize roses…
C, LONDON

LADY EXPOSES BAD BOYFRIEND

When my best friend told me that my boyfriend was sleeping around I plotted revenge. He had been hassling me for anal sex, so one evening I told him I would only let him if he dressed in women's clothes and let me tie him to the bed. After I gave him a makeover, I tied him up with my stockings, then told him I had to go and get the lubricant. He didn't know, but I'd invited our mates round for a party, so went to let them in and told them to go into the room where my boyfriend was lying on the bed with an erection, make-up, stockings and suspenders!
TAMARA, VIA E-MAIL

Out for a meal, my mother-in-law was asked by the waiter whether she wanted her pizza cut into four or six slices. "Four," she said. "I couldn't possibly manage six."

My housemate read a fashion feature about how everyone was wearing crosses these days. "I've worn one for ages!" she exclaimed. I pointed out that it was because of her religious beliefs, not for fashion. "Not true," she replied. "If I wanted to do that, I'd wear one with a little man on it."

While discussing how shit Big Brother was, my flatmate quipped, "If only it were more like the 1984 version…" His girlfriend replied, "Was that the first series, then?"

While working as an office temp my sister had to type up an illegible handwritten letter which came from the County Chief Executive. Unfortunately, she used her "initiative" – and signed off his title as "Country Chef Executioner".

OFFICE GIRL TREATS BOSS

One weekend, my boyfriend and I had to go into my office to pick something up. Of course, it was deserted, and both feeling horny we decided to get down to it on my desk. After the deed was done we realised we'd left a sizeable pool of love juices next to my computer, so we grabbed a nearby sponge and cleared it up. The following Monday at work it gave me great satisfaction to kindly volunteer to wash up my cretin of a boss's mug and serve him up some special protein-rich tea!
CAROLINE, ENFIELD

Cheat gets hurt

A few years ago while walking home one night from our local pub, me and my then-boyfriend Tim both felt a bit horny and decided to find somewhere to have a shag. We went to a nearby park and Tim thought it would be a good idea to do it on the centre spot of the football pitch. After about 20 minutes of frantic sex we left and finished off at his house. In the morning he had to play football so I went along to watch. During the game Tim spotted the condom we had used the night before and picked it up to show me. Just then the ball went flying into his face and there was an awful crack. Later on I found out that the prick had been cheating on me so I dumped him. But I still get massive satisfaction whenever I see him with his now-wife down the pub, wearing the most crooked nose I have ever seen.

TINA, VIA E-MAIL

JIGGY COUPLE PARK UP

After a hot and heavy trip to the movies, my bloke suggested we go for a drive. I happily agreed as I was gagging for it. We drove out to what we thought was a secluded spot down a woodland road, turned the engine off and moved to the back seat. Immediately I unzipped his jeans and started sucking his cock; he happily returned the favour, putting one leg on the parcel shelf and licking me out. After I came he leaned me over the rear seat and took me from behind. We were at it for five minutes when some headlights approached. I didn't stop pushing on to his cock but the lights seemed to stay on for ages. Suddenly there was a tap on the window. My boyfriend wound it down and an embarrassed old lady said, "Excuse me, but could you move as you're blocking my driveway?" I couldn't stop giggling as we hastily drove away.
SALLY, VIA E-MAIL

LADIES GET FAMILIAR

The other day I went to my boyfriend's house but his 24-year-old sister answered the door and told me he wouldn't be in until later because he was playing football. She asked me if I wanted to stay for a few drinks while I waited so I said yes and went inside. Pretty soon we'd gone through two bottles of wine and she was asking me if my sex life was any good. At first I was embarrassed but decided, mainly thanks to the alcohol, to tell her every dirty detail of sex with her brother. After hearing my filth she said out of the blue that she bet she could give me multiple orgasms if I let her. I giggled and said okay. We made our way to her bed and slowly took each other's clothes off. After much feverish kissing and fondling I went down on her, pulling the bed quilt over me, and proceeded to lick her clit while sliding three fingers into her soaking wet pussy. However, to our horror, my boyfriend had returned home without either of us knowing. He knocked on his sister's door and before she could say anything he came in and witnessed a mysterious figure going down on her under the covers. He apologised and quickly shut the door. I sneaked out the house and the next day he told me what he'd seen, calling his sister a "dirty cow". If only he knew…

LISA, LONDON

GIRL INTERRUPTED

One day I got home from work early, the first time in months that I'd arrived there before my boyfriend. Relishing some time on my own I decided to pleasure myself on the sofa. During a luscious naked frig I was almost reaching climax when I heard my boyfriend arrive home. Hoping that he'd continue the fun I shouted for him to come in and join me, only to get a little more than I'd bargained for. He'd brought back a load of his workmates to have beer and watch football. Oops.

NICHOLA, EDINBURGH

COUPLE BORROW MORE THAN BED

One night, me and my then-boyfriend were keeping a friend company while her mum and dad were away. After shitloads to drink, we decided to call it a night. My friend gave me and my fella her room while she slept in her parents' bed. When we got to the room, after all the vodka, we were both as horny as hell and got down to some serious shagging. Then my bloke grabbed the nearest thing to him to "insert" into me for pleasure. It turned out to be my mate's hairbrush which got covered in my hot love juices. We didn't think anything of it until the next morning when she came into the room,

Out of the mouths of babes

A former girlfriend was always trying to take a photo of the beautiful sunsets on Ascension Island, but most evenings was foiled by the weather. "Doesn't the sun ever set in front of the clouds?" she asked me eventually.

grabbed the brush to do her hair, and stuck it, handle first, in her mouth while she tied her hair back! Yummy for her!

KELLY, VIA E-MAIL

EXERCISE BENEFICIAL

In the last couple of months I've realised how much fun going to the gym can be. That's because I've discovered that there are two things that can give me an amazing orgasm – sit-ups and doing my calf muscles on the machine! I wonder if anyone has noticed yet – perhaps they think those groans are of pain and not pure pleasure! Should get down the gym more often…

STACEY, VIA E-MAIL

CONVENT GIRL RUDER THAN EVER

As a teenager I went to a Catholic school and it was those years that taught me all I know about being a naughty girl. Anyway, a few weeks ago my bloke was out, so I organised for my old schoolmate, Hannah, to come round. Soon we were legless! Remembering "old times", we stripped down to our underwear, got out my old camcorder and stumbled into bed. We began sensually touching each other, but soon it was a lot more. When we couldn't find my dildo, Han began fucking me with the nearest thing to hand – my crucifix! Phew! Some weeks after these disgraceful scenes my boyfriend found the tape. To his surprise there were two naked chicks on his video – he was well chuffed and thanked me for a massive turn-on. Don't mention it!

ANON, VIA E-MAIL

FHM E-MAIL RUINS LIFE

I'd been planning to send FHM my confession involving lingerie, a champagne bottle and an orgasm for a while, but it's ended up causing me grief. I originally tried to e-mail my confession from my home computer at my parents' house. Due to a spelling error in the address the e-mail was returned as undelivered into the family inbox, which I later discovered my father read. I'm sending this from my boyfriend's computer.

SARAH, VIA E-MAIL

Ladies' Confessions

Visiting the place where Irish martyr Michael Collins was shot, my sister asked why he didn't take cover behind the memorial when they were shooting at him.

After remarking to my mate's bird that it was nice to see the sun and the moon in the sky at the same time, she told me: "Don't be stupid! How can that happen? They're the same thing."

During the Jubilee weekend my girlfriend piped up, "Why does Prince Charles always hang around with the Queen?" When I'd picked myself off the floor, she confirmed that she hadn't realised the two were related.

While I was sanding down a piece of wood my girlfriend watched, amazed. "I didn't know that wood was made from little pieces of dust," she explained afterwards.

I took my girlfriend for her first experience of watching football at the pub. The place was packed and all was going well, until Tony Adams put his hand on the mascot's shoulder. "What position does that little man play in?" she asked, loudly.

TECHNOLOGY AIDS LUST

When my husband was sent off to Bosnia for six months we prepared for the separation by investing in a pair of picture phones. The "private" pictures we exchanged were good, but they didn't replace everything I was missing. After two months of my man's absence, I met a guy from work I quite fancied. He came round to my place one night, and after a while we got down to sex. While we were doing the deed he suggested I take some pics. The closest thing to hand was the phone, so I took 10 shots of really steamy stuff. Chatting to my hubby the next day, he asked me to send him some "nice" snaps of myself. When I did, he sent me back some of him wanking, asking me to send him some more. It was then I realised that I'd inadvertently sent a couple of pics of me and my work colleague at it. But my hubby loved it! Phew!

SUZANNE, GERMANY

LADY MAKES FILTH TAPE

The city-centre studio I run has an exit in a small alley that we cover with CCTV. Whenever friends talk about spicing up their sex lives I always suggest an outdoor session in the alley behind where I work because "it's very secluded and I've done it loads of times". Every morning I fast forward through the tape and make a copy of any open-air sessions – currently I've over two hours of friends and complete strangers getting a seeing-to, completely oblivious to the camera and even more oblivious to the fact my late nights at work usually consist of masturbating to said tape.

JJ, VIA E-MAIL

GIRLS GET LESBO

For ages my boyfriend has been asking me to fulfill his fantasy – lesbian sex. Anyway, one night while at a party at his mate's, I had this girl coming on to me. Shortly after my fella asked me if I fancied her. After a few more drinks I'd had enough and stomped off to the toilet. While in the loo, the same girl walked in and started chatting. I told her I knew my boyfriend had set me up and we both had a laugh about it. It was then I decided to teach my man a lesson. I slid my hand between her legs and started fingering her. Before I knew it we ended up doing each other all around the bathroom – it was the best sex ever. But the best bit is that I've now split up with him and am moving in with Shelly in a fortnight! Thanks for everything, mate, you were right – I didn't know what I was missing.

TRACEY, MANCHESTER

Fellas do some experimenting

Some months ago me and a female pal were staying at a hotel in Chester. After a meal and vats of wine we got chatting to some sexy blokes at the bar. Soon enough we were all off to our room where we had a little orgy – which was great until one of the guys said to the other, "This is great Hywel, much better than just you and me, eh?" Absolutely true.
ANN, CONSETT

SISTER GETS EYEFUL

Many years ago, when I was a teenager and still living at home, I went to ask my brother if I could borrow an album of his. I dutifully knocked on his bedroom door and upon the shouted reply, "Come in," went in, only to see him shoot his load all over his girlfriend who lay, spread out naked, underneath his bouncing form. I quickly realised that what he'd shouted was his intentions to his girlfriend and not instructions to me! I quietly left without either of them ever knowing.
SUSAN, VIA E-MAIL

LEZZERS GIVE PRICELESS SHOW

One night, after a particularly drunken uni evening, me and my girlfriend decided to retire to my boudoir for a little rough and tumble. As soon as the door shut we were on the bed,

69-ing the night away. Suddenly I heard a funny noise from the next room. Being that our walls are about as thick as toilet roll, I soon realised the gimpy guy next door was beating himself off at the sounds of our furious orgasms. My girlfriend then suggested we should visit our neighbour. So off we went, stark naked, to knock on his door. With jaw on the floor and a lump in his trousers, we pushed the spotty freak onto the bed and stripped him down. Unfortunately, being an obviously inexperienced chappy, it was only a few seconds before he'd shot his load, so me and my girlfriend decided to finish each other off, to a thunderous climax. Now we can't help but smirk as the pizza-faced fool tries in vain to boast about his conquest to all and sundry, who merely scoff and call him a lying twat. If only they knew...

V, NORWICH

SEX TOY VENGEANCE

My ex-boyfriend and I decided to spice up our sex life so we bought a "Tickler Set" from our local sex shop. When it arrived I eagerly opened the box but my dog thought it was a toy and kept trying to snatch it out of my hand. In the end I had to put it away in a drawer. Later that week I found out that my bloke had been sleeping with my mate, so when he next came round I took him upstairs to try on one of the Tickler thingies. I waited until he'd put it on his cock and then let my dog into the bedroom. She took one look at it, and thinking it was some sort of toy for her to rip to shreds, jumped up and bit him on his cock! Ahh, revenge...

CARRIE, BRISTOL

LUSH REVEALS A LITTLE TOO MUCH

It was my second year at university and a boozy Freshers' week. One night I reached my full potential by beating the lads' rugby team in a drinking competition on stage. Later on I somehow found my way home to discover my (mostly male) flatmates in the lounge. As I slumped in the corner, one asked me what I'd done to my knee. This confused me, but when I looked down what I saw made me sprint to the toilet. What had happened was that my sanitary towel had slipped down inside my tights and was resting on my knee. The worst thing is that I still don't know whether or not it was there while I was on stage in front of hundreds of fellow students!

PAM, VIA E-MAIL

COUSINS DO MORE THAN KISS

For a while now, I've been fantasising about anal sex. However, as my husband isn't brave enough to explore the "other passage", I had resigned myself to life as an anal virgin. Then, at a drunken family get-together, my younger cousin was telling me how he'd never managed to persuade any girlfriend to let him try anal. My eyes lit up, and I persuaded him to walk me home that night, as my husband was away. Once home, I explained that we shared a similar predicament, and, after a little persuasion, got him to bugger me on the couch. It was well worth waiting for, and the fact that we were related only added to the excitement. We now meet up regularly for anal sessions.

TRACEY, YORKSHIRE

GAMBLERS GO FOR IT

My boyfriend and I have our little thing called "the one-minute gamble", which means, when we're in my flat, say in the kitchen, and my flatmates are in the house, we time ourselves doing something rude for exactly one minute. It's an amazing turn-on! He might hoist me onto a bench, pull my panties aside and lick me out, or just give me a quick knobbing from behind. I think he's gutted that we haven't been caught yet! I'm pretty sure we'll soon be doing "the two-minute gamble"…

KATH, SWISS COTTAGE

NAUGHTY LADY IMPROVISES

My now ex-boyfriend came to my works do with me. We were sitting on a table of about 30 people when I noticed a guy I fancied in the office at the opposite end making eyes at me. I like to tease so I discreetly played along. Between courses I excused myself and went to the ladies. However, the guy followed me and

Out of the mouths of babes

Trying to impress a female colleague with the wonders of the internet, I popped her postcode into an aerial mapping website and zoomed down onto her house. Bemused, she asked how come she could see her car sitting in the drive when it was clearly parked in our car park. Laugh? I nearly sacked her.

Watching the Stallone movie *Cliffhanger* on TV the other night, we came to the part where a man is hanging from a tree as a pack of hungry hounds nibble on his shoe. My lovely girlfriend innocently asked, "Are they rescue wolves?"

On our descent into Dublin airport at 25,000ft, my wife pointed down at the bay. "You can see the fish jumping!" she said with girlish glee. Sadly, I had to inform her that she was looking at ferries.

Riveted by the Grand Prix live on telly the other week, my girlfriend sent the entire room into hysterics by commenting, "Do they stop racing when the adverts come on?" Sad but true.

pulled me – willingly, I might add – into a cubicle in the gents. He bent me over and lifted my dress, ripping off my G-string. We started going at it like rabbits when through the crack of the door I saw someone come into the toilet. To my shock – and excitement – it was my boyfriend! Luckily the guy put his hand over my mouth, as I then had a great orgasm while watching my oblivious boyfriend! After he left, we waited a few minutes and then made our exit. I joined my boyfriend at the table looking a little flushed! The guy followed a few minutes

later and as I glanced up I could see him wiping his mouth with what appeared to be a table napkin. But it was my very moist G-string! Later on I had to make something up, so told my boyfriend that just to tease him I hadn't worn any knickers. He was so horny thinking about it that I had his cock in me on the way home!
GEMMA, BRISTOL

SAUCY TALE GETS GIRL GOING

I went to stay with my best girl mate and one night we went out clubbing where I met this really nice guy. After a couple of hours of "getting to know each other" he and I sneaked into the loos and I wanked him off. When I was walking home with my mate later (just slightly tipsy), she admitted she'd got really wet when thinking about what my guy and I had got up to. By the time we got to her place we were so horny we 69'd on the floor in her living

Out of the mouths of babes

Approaching Glasgow Airport in the car last year, my wife was getting excited at the prospect of flying. "Wow!" she exclaimed. "Aren't the planes low when they're coming in to land!"

While at a friend's house, her mate came in, unplugged the phone and jacked her own phone in. "I'm expecting an important phone call," she explained.

My girlfriend and I were talking about doing a bungee jump. I wondered whether they lowered the rope down when the jump was over, or winched you back to the top. My girl replied, "Don't you jump, bounce up and land on the platform again?"

room. First time with another girl, but I'm certainly ready to put on a show with her for any guy who asks...
LIX, VIA E-MAIL

ANGRY GIRLFRIEND SUITS HERSELF

A few years back I was going out with a guy who loved every type of sex going. After trying almost everything there was only one thing left to do – a threesome! I was more than willing so we went everywhere to get another woman, but no joy. Then I received a phone call from his sister saying he'd been seeing other women behind my back. So as I was down in the dumps I went to my friend's house and we started getting drunk. Then her boyfriend turned up, and as the night went on we started talking about sex and all got horny. So she suggested a threesome! We were all willing and it was fantastic. But the best of it was a week later when my so-called boyfriend turned up. My friend stood up and said, "Have you told him about the other night?" I was shocked at first by what she said but then I told him everything – his face was a picture. It felt great. Then I slept with his brother, but that's another story.
MH, MANCHESTER

ENDOWED HELPER BOPS VICTIM

While on holiday with my then-boyfriend in Greece we were sitting by the pool when the man next to us fell down and started having a fit. I knew first aid, so jumped out my seat and started to move stuff out of the way so he didn't injure himself. Just as I bent over, the catch on my bikini top came undone and my FFs fell out and hit him in the face. I was so embarrassed I made a run for it!
YVONNE, GLASGOW

BLOKE TAKES SLEEPY SEX TOO FAR

My ex-boyfriend and I were going through a bit of a sexual drought, mostly because he was always too stoned to do anything. One night, when my fella thought I was asleep, he started going down on me. I was too pissed off with him to stir, so pretended to be still asleep. Next

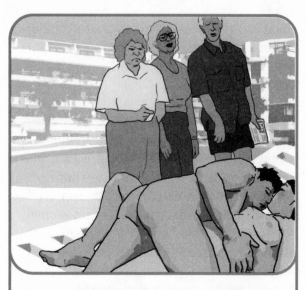

Eyeful for oldies

Unable to afford a holiday abroad, my parents offered to take myself and my boyfriend with them to Benidorm. Craving the sun we agreed. Upon arrival we discovered we were allocated to a hotel with nobody under 50 in sight! On top of this we had to have the living room in my parents' apartment. Not happy, we decided to make the most of it and go and get sloshed. After many cocktails we decided we would have more privacy making out in the hotel pool, which was now closed. As it was all oldies in the hotel we decided it would be safe. After a period of passionate love-making we dragged ourselves out of the pool and lay naked on some sun loungers to dry off in case my parents heard us coming in. Unfortunately the alcohol took over and before we knew it we were awoken, at 9am, by a group of OAPs shouting how disgusting it was and calling for their rep.

ANGELA, MIDDLESBROUGH

thing I know, he's on top of me, having sex. I'm ashamed to admit I found it a bit of a turn-on, so didn't say anything. This happened for a few nights – I just pretended to be asleep, he shagged me silly and we were both happy. Obviously, though, the novelty soon wore off. I had to put an end to it after one

night, when he thought I was asleep, he shoved my finger up his arse and began wanking... Had to say enough is enough then, I'm afraid.
NICKY, VIA E-MAIL

SPOUSE GETS IT VERY WRONG

My husband and I were at a party and he was accusing me of making eyes at every guy that was there. I went to the toilet to calm down and on leaving saw a girl I used to know from school. I told her what had happened and she dried my tears, then gave me a kiss on the cheek which turned into a full-on snog with her tongue. We returned to the ladies where I had the most fantastic oral sex with tongues and even fingers probing my little starfish. I still haven't told my husband that it's not the guys he has to worry about.
SH, WALES

QUICKIE GOES YUCKY

On a Saturday night out with some mates I was approached by a really sexy guy in a bar. After some polite chit-chat we stumbled into a taxi back to his pad where very soon we began humping like wild animals in his bed. After some time he went down on me and gave me some full-on, mind-blowing tongue action. Losing control I accidentally broke wind in his face, causing him to throw up all over me. I was so mortified and humiliated that I decided not to stick around to wipe his chin...
CLARE, STOKE ON TRENT

CAMPING GETS SUPER-RUDE

I went on this camping trip with my girlfriends and some blokes. One night we all got drunk around the campfire and after a while me and my friend invited my boyfriend and his mate into a tent. It soon got a bit steamy and my mate asked the guys if they'd all fancy a kissing three-way. They readily agreed and tongues were soon everywhere, with my boyfriend making out with my best mate. I was just watching when his friend invited me in – I thought, Payback! Thirty minutes later my boyfriend was passed out pissed on the floor of the tent. Seeing the opportunity, his friend asked me to strip, so I did, nice and slowly to tease him. First he fingered me, then he started giving it to me doggy style as I screamed with pleasure. I thought this was great – cheating on my boyfriend with his best friend while he's two feet away. In the morning I asked him if he remembered anything. He replied, "I can remember two people shagging close by, but I don't know who they were." Perfect.

"YOUNG 'UN", SCOTLAND

SEXED-UP MINX CAUSES MISCHIEF

One evening I was waiting for my boyfriend to return home from a few days working away, so I thought I'd get myself in the mood ready for his return. I decided to watch one of his "special videos" and test out the new vibrator he'd kindly bought me for Christmas. After several intense orgasms I heard his car pull into the drive. As he came in the door I didn't give him the chance to refuse and, completely naked, pushed him to the floor, undid his trousers and jumped straight on top of him. Then as I was leaping up and down in ecstasy I heard this almighty crack. My boyfriend screamed and I leapt off to discover I'd broken his ribs with my exertions. He then had to go around telling everyone he'd done it at football training.

TANYA, CAMBRIDGESHIRE

LADY MISHEARS LOVER

During a hot one-night stand, the bloke I was with breathlessly asked me to do a "waterfall". Being more than happy to experiment I smiled, asked him to roll on to his front and then pissed all over his back. Turns out he actually just said I was "beautiful"…

VICKY, WEST YORKSHIRE

HOLIDAY LOVE GETS STICKY

Last summer, I went back to this guy's apartment in Faliraki for sex. After a couple of shags he started wanking, then came all over my stomach. Which would have been okay, but he then started licking it all up! And then licked my face with his spunky tongue! Bye bye Mr Weirdo…

RACHAEL, BIRMINGHAM

SOLDIER DOES DAMAGE

Me and my fiancé wanted to have some spicy sex as he was being sent to Iraq for God knows how long. A friend had told us about her boyfriend putting one of those mint things that melt on your tongue onto her clit while he licked her pussy. So, one night during a session, my bloke placed the mint strip on my love button. At first it felt cold, then hot, but I was enjoying the tongue action that I was receiving. Then it started to burn... a lot. I screamed and attempted to move away from his thrusting tongue but he misunderstood and thought that I was really enjoying it, saying things like, "You love it, you dirty little minx!" In the end I had to push him off me just to get him to stop! I've

Out of the mouths of babes

One of my lovely girlfriend's colleagues was reviewing a book by immobile computer-voiced physicist Stephen Hawking. Stumped on the first sentence, she asked my girlfriend, "Is he American?" He's English, she replied. The girl wasn't sure, and said, "I've seen him on TV and he's got an American accent."

On Gran Canaria with my girlfriend, I noticed a man doing a spot of paragliding. "I bet he's having a great time up there in the thermals," I said. "Don't be stupid," she replied. "I'm sure they wear wetsuits."

A girl I know was showing me the "Stars & Stripes" bikini she'd bought for her Australian holiday. I said it was a shame she wasn't going to the US. "Don't worry," she told me, "Australia uses the same flag." She qualifies as a doctor in ten months.

never been in so much pain – I couldn't sit down for a week. All I can say is that my mate must have a clit made out of leather!

VICKY, VIA E-MAIL

GIRL GETS ACQUAINTED WITH DAD

I'd been seeing this guy for two months and although he bought me everything I wanted, he was a real bore. His dad, on the other hand, was very different and much more sexually attractive. So I thought I'd try it on with him when my boyfriend was out getting us a take-away. I crept upstairs and into his room. Seconds later he came in and before he said anything I told him to be quiet, shut the door and lick my pussy. Without protest he did as he was told and was soon taking me from behind and in all my pleasure I didn't see my boyfriend standing there in front of me! Expecting tantrums and accepting the fact that I would have to pay for my own stuff from now on, I was surprised when he got his todger out and urged me to take it in my mouth. During the double whamming I realised that maybe I had been wrong, because, in this respect at least, it certainly was like father, like son.

LUCY, LONDON

... AND ANOTHER GETS ACQUAINTED WITH MUM

My then-boyfriend and I were out for his birthday and I had plans to take him home for a real birthday treat – but he wanted to continue drinking with his mates. I stormed off, but on the way home decided to go to his house, where he lived with his mum, to wait for him. She let me in and offered a sympathetic ear and a drink. After a few glasses of wine I was pretty drunk, so when his mum's hand started working its way up my leg I didn't complain and soon enjoyed the best oral sex I have ever had. To this day, he still doesn't know what happened.

ALEX, YORK

RELAXING NIGHT ENDS IN CHAOS

After a hard day at work, I wanted to get back to my boyfriend's house, have a long bath and go to sleep. After the bath things got heated, and my boyfriend decided it would be a good idea to use an after shave bottle on me. Not only did the lid come off inside off me, but his little brother and his friend walked in when he was trying to fish it out. Bugger...

HEATHER, SCOTLAND

HAPLESS HUSBAND GETS WELCOME-HOME "PRESENT"

Me and my husband's sex life was pretty boring until the time I got home from work early. My husband came back on time, but I'd decided to have a little fun by myself. He caught me ramming my dildo in myself – with a nappy and bonnet on! Which surprised him.

ROSALIND, NEWPORT

HORNY HOLIDAYMAKER HAS DOUBLE THE FUN

On holiday in the Balearics last summer, I was with my boyfriend but I'd been flirting with a group of German lads who were staying in our hotel. One afternoon as my boyfriend lay by the pool, I decided to hit the shops. As I left our room I met two of the German guys. They were laden with sangria and asked if I'd join them on their balcony for a drink. After a couple of strong sangrias I was feeling a little drunk and horny as the guys were lying naked on either side of me. I thought, What the hell, I'm on holiday, go for it! So there I was, on a balcony, 15 stories above the pool where my man was laying – being spit-roasted! I was in so much ecstasy that I couldn't help howling like a dog as the guys rammed me from all directions! Returning

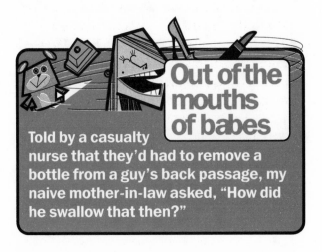

Out of the mouths of babes

Told by a casualty nurse that they'd had to remove a bottle from a guy's back passage, my naive mother-in-law asked, "How did he swallow that then?"

Extra-helpful assistant plugs panties

One day when I worked at the lingerie shop my sister was manager of, a good-looking guy came in and started perusing the stock. After looking at half our stock he still wasn't happy, so with a wicked look in his eye said to me, "You look like you wear nice underwear. What you got on?" Since we were in the quiet back bit of the shop, I lifted up my skirt to show him my sexy – and see-through – knickers. After a good, long look he said, "Right, I'll have those please." After selling a similar set to him, I was so turned on I went to the loo and wanked myself silly.

"J", SOMERSET

to the pool my fella was eager to tell me I missed the funniest thing. Apparently while I was away everybody was in hysterics listening to some tart being given a good seeing-to and barking like a dog on heat somewhere up above.

SANDY, VIA E-MAIL

BEAU SHOWN THE RED CARD

My boyfriend has a fetish for feet. One evening my mother invited us round for tea but made the mistake of taking her sandals off. My boyfriend couldn't take his eyes off her feet, so after tea when we were washing up, I told him off. A little later I went upstairs to use the loo and as I was a bit horny spent a while there. When I eventually returned, my boyfriend had gone. I asked my mum why and she replied he'd told her what lovely feet she had and asked her to have a threesome with the two of us! She'd slapped him and kicked him out, and I ain't heard from him since.

SUE, EXETER

WAITER PROVIDES SOLID SERVICE

During a girls' weekend in Amsterdam, we went to a really dubious nightclub featuring naked waiters and waitresses. One waiter took a fancy to me and as the demon drink began to take hold I started to get more daring with him. As we were sat in a poorly lit corner I took a chance and made a gentle grab for his cock. He didn't bat an eyelid and just stood there while I continued to stroke it. It didn't take long before he became aroused. It was obvious he didn't want me to stop so he turned around to face the wall and soon reached orgasm and left a sizeable deposit on the wall. He quickly composed himself and walked away to continue waiting on others. It took me considerably longer to stop shaking.

BEA, GREENFORD

WEEKEND WORKER IS GIVEN SECRET TREAT

While at uni, I worked weekends at an estate agents. I was often left alone, which I saw as an ideal opportunity for spending on my boss's desk in the back room while my boyfriend gave me a good shagging. I'll never forget the time when we moved into the main office, where he sat himself between my legs under my desk and proceeded to give my pussy a licking as I went about making phone calls. All was fine until my boss walked in – we both froze! She didn't stay for long, but it was the most mortifying, but strangely arousing, five minutes of my life, what with the cheeky bugger flicking my pussy with his tongue as I talked to her.

EMMA, MANCHESTER

Ladies' Confessions

Out of the mouths of babes

Visiting Ireland recently, a friend took the wife and I on a coastal tour. "They call this U-Boat Rock," he told us. "It looks more like a submarine," replied the wife, quick as a flash.

Driving into town I had to stop at a railway crossing. As the barrier closed, my girlfriend's mate asked why there was a bell ringing. "So blind drivers know when to stop," replied my lovely girlfriend.

Surfing the internet, I asked my girlfriend to go to the FHM website. She paused before asking, "How do you spell FHM?" Oh, and she's studying for a degree!

EMBARRASSMENT FOR HORNY COUPLE

One night me and my ex-bloke stayed at his parents' to look after their house. After a while we got bored so I unzipped him and started to give him a juicy blow-job. We didn't realise how late it was so when the door opened and his parents walked in on us I jolted up in shock, only to find my boyfriend jumping up as well, forcing my top lip into the zipper of his jeans. It got much worse. His mother then had to try and free my lip away from the zip, with her son's limp cock still in my mouth, unable to be taken out until my lip was free. Funnily enough I was never invited round again!
ANON, VIA E-MAIL

SWINGER SURPRISED

My husband and I used to enjoy swinging. One time we hooked up with a guy called Mike, who was pretty nervous about the whole thing. We tried to make Mike comfortable and offered him some wine and nibbles. After a while he perked up a bit, so casually unbuttoning his trousers, I released his throbbing hard-on. My lips were soon tracing his cock with supple kisses. My partner leaned over Mike's shoulder taking Polaroids, then went to recline on the sofa. I carried on dragging my lips down Mike's shaft, then felt something lightly brush my cheek. I opened my eyes to see what it was. I did a double take – Mike was casually eating Pringles while I sucked him off! My husband was in stitches – I was furious. Mike was soon shown the door…

C, OXFORDSHIRE

LADY LIVES FANTASY

One of my fantasies is to be taken by two cocks at the same time, so knowing how liberal-minded my man is I let him into my secret. The next night I turned up at his place to find him and his best mate waiting for me, pants bulging. Neither of them could take their eyes off me as I stripped down to my G-string and told them to wrestle each other for my snatch. The sight of their rock-hard cocks pressed against straining muscles soon had my pussy dripping wet. Desperate for cock I squeezed in between them, straddling my man while he pulled apart my butt cheeks for his friend to enter me from behind. It was the best ride of my life. Now I'm looking for a hot woman to help fulfill my man's fantasy… the two of us oiled up in thongs wrestling over his cock.

SARAH, CORNWALL

AFTER-HOURS SHENANIGANS CAUGHT ON FILM

I used to work in an agency in the City. One night after a leaving party, my boss, who I fancied, shared a cab home with me. We stopped off at the office on the way back because he needed to pick something up. As we were leaving he said he really fancied me, so I took the opportunity and kissed him. I then started undoing his trousers, got on my knees and gave him a wicked blow-job. When I arrived at work the next morning there were police everywhere – some drunk had smashed the front window of the office. The CCTV footage was next to be checked; to my horror the video was played and there I was, butt-naked spread across the table on all fours, noshing my boss off!

ANEETA, VIA E-MAIL

SEX TOY MISHAP

A few months back my boyfriend and I decided to have a hot, horny night in. After taking turns at teasing and pleasing he handcuffed me to the spindles on the staircase and took control, using

Out of the mouths of babes

Watching TV, the film *Event Horizon* was coming up. My girlfriend asked what it was about. I explained it was set in the future, when some professor goes mental aboard a spaceship and kills people. "Is it a true story?" she said.

old faithful Rampant Rabbit. Sitting naked and hard between my legs, he pumped the vibrator into my pussy. He was then hit by a few drops of liquid, and thinking that I was on the verge of exploding he kept going. Unfortunately it wasn't me about to explode but the battery. The drops were the acid from inside which had landed smack on the head of his member! As he rushed to the bathroom to wash it off I was left helpless and laughing, still handcuffed.

JULIE, CUMBRIA

LEWD LAD TAUGHT LESSON

A few months ago I was in a club with my then boyfriend and his mates. I was on my fifth JD and Coke when my boyfriend's only good-looking mate started flirting with me. Feeling very horny I told my bloke to meet me in the ladies in five minutes for a treat. As soon as he was in the cubicle I was on my knees giving him a terrific blow-job. After a few minutes I heard a muffled laugh, and looking up I saw two of his goons laughing like mad. The prick had told them to come and watch his dirty woman in action. With me feeling very pissed-off back at the bar, the good-looking friend told me how he tried to talk them out of it. Seizing the opportunity to get back at my shitty boyfriend, I took his mate to the same cubicle where he proceeded to bend me over and give me the best shag of my life!

CAROL, SURREY

COUNTRY GIRL HAS SPECIAL DAY

This summer I woke up one morning and in my horny state thought, I'm going to spend the whole day in the nude! My parents were away and we live in a remote part of the countryside, so it wasn't going to be too much of a problem. And so I cooked naked, sunbathed naked, watched telly naked… and frigged myself silly naked – lots! Towards the end of the day I wanted to take a risk, so did the short walk to the local postbox without wearing a single stitch. Just as I was returning I heard a car approaching, so slowed down a wee bit and made sure the driver, whoever he might be, saw my cute bum before I disappeared inside! Cue a lot more wanking indoors. I'll have to do this again next summer…

MANDA, DEVON

DAUGHTER KEEPS FAMILY TRADITIONS GOING

I live with my parents, and recently my boyfriend came to spend the day with me. We soon escaped into my room to watch films. Not long into the movie I felt very horny and it wasn't long before we were having great, passionate sex. But just before my bloke came… my mum walked in! He jumped off me, pulling up his jeans as my mum asked what the hell was going on. At this point I jumped on top of my man and began tickling him, making out that was what we'd been up to all along. For the next few days my mum gave us some horrible glares. To be frank I don't see her problem. We all know about the stash of porn videos, luminous condoms and vibrator under her bed.

LORI, VIA E-MAIL

House tour gets steamy

My fella and I moved into a new house and got engaged around the same time, so we invited all our mates round for a celebration. They brought lots of champagne and I was soon well and truly smashed. I was showing my fella's best female mate drunkenly around the house, when we somehow got onto a conversation about "lady love". Imagine my surprise when, by the time we reached the attic room, we were tearing each other's clothes off. We screwed like mad right there on the floor and then returned to the party as though nothing had happened! Waving my fingers under my fella's nose, I whispered in his ear, "Guess what I've been doing!"

SD, CHESHIRE

BATHTIME GETS YUCKY

When I was ill once, my boyfriend suggested we have a nice bath together, which would "make me feel better". So we both got in, me with my back to him in between his legs. We were in there for quite some while and it started to get cold so I lent forward to turn on the hot tap, when I let out the biggest fart you could possibly imagine. I expected my boyfriend to laugh but instead he leapt up with a loud yell and jumped

Out of the mouths of babes

Out walking on a hot summer's day with my girlfriend, we saw some bin-men lugging dripping bags of rubbish across the road. "I don't fancy their job..." I commented. "Yeah, but they only work one day a week," she replied.

out of the bath. To my horror I realised I hadn't just farted but in my ill state I had also followed through and it was now floating all around me! We weren't a couple for long after that.

C, NORTHAMPTON

BUBBLE-BATH CLEVERNESS

My boyfriend and I were taking a bath and I just couldn't keep my hands off his cock. So after a few gentle strokes I got it exactly how I like it, rock hard. I love giving him blow-jobs, so in he went! I'd emptied my fella the previous night but when he came there was a bucketload. Proud of the overflowing contents I had just taken into my mouth, I opened my gob to reveal all. With that, I coughed and blew a huge bubble of come through my nose. Thankfully there was plenty left to swallow.

A, HULL

HOLIDAY SHAG DISASTER

My friend and I went on a girlie holiday to Torquay. After a cocktail-fuelled night I pulled this bloke who was also the worse for wear. As I was feeling horny I decided to go for it, so he led me to a grotty stairwell in a car park where he gave me the worst 15-second shag of my life. Then, to my horror, I discovered the condom was "lost" inside me! It took a lot longer to fish out than he'd spent shagging me. And after all my contortions I looked up to see a security camera pointing straight at me. It then actually moved and followed my descent down the stairs.

P, PORTSMOUTH

CHAMBERMAID GETS DOUBLE SURPRISE

I am a chambermaid in a city-centre hotel. One morning I was servicing a bedroom when I found a dirty magazine, so I had a flick through and started touching myself. Suddenly the door opened and the guest walked in. To my surprise he shut the door and joined in. He was well equipped and was soon skillfully spearing me with his hefty cock. I later confessed to my now ex-boyfriend, who was not too impressed.

TC, VIA E-MAIL

LOO SHENANIGANS HALTED

For our anniversary my boyfriend and I decided to have a romantic meal out. Once we got to the restaurant, we couldn't keep our hands off each other and a tingle rose inside me, tickling my pussy. I couldn't control myself and had to rush to the toilets, telling my boyfriend to follow shortly. As I burst through the toilet to check the all clear, I pulled him in and he pushed me into the nearest cubicle. We were getting down to it, when I heard a familiar voice. It was the voice of my mother, pulling my father seductively into the toilets! They'd obviously had the same idea when out for a meal. Sure enough it killed the passion and we left extremely unsatisfied.

DANIELLE, NEWCASTLE

BUS JOURNEY BRIGHTENED UP

One day my boyfriend called me when I was on the back seat of the bus and started talking really dirty. It'd been a pretty boring ride before that, but now I unbuttoned some of the buttons on my dress and started to play with myself. I fiddled with my clit for a good half hour and came heaps of times. It was a great feeling knowing I could get caught at any time! My boyfriend loved what I was doing and shortly after came round my house and gave me a damn good shagging.

SSB, VIA E-MAIL

COUPLE VARY THINGS

One night me and my husband decided to attempt something different – a spot of anal sex. With both our children sleeping in the next

Out of the mouths of babes

On *Walking With Dinosaurs*, one of the creatures was dying on a beach, looking as if it was in extreme pain. "Can't the camera crew do anything to help?" my girlfriend piped up.

A female friend of mine was shown a blow-up sex doll at a party. Noticing the rounded, cavernous mouth, she blurted out: "Eeew! That wouldn't be very nice to kiss."

Out shopping with my girlfriend, we bought a copy of the Big Issue. The vendor told us it was his last one. "You can go home now," my girl informed him, helpfully.

room we thought it'd be safe. After my husband got me really horny it was time to insert the python. It took a great deal of time trying to get it in, but finally we managed, with me on all fours on the bed. We were at it for ages groaning and moaning, then my eye caught something at the side of me. It was my six-year-old just standing there! I had to explain myself by saying that daddy and I were playing cowboys and Indians. Thankfully he wasn't traumatised, but the next morning he asked me who won the game of cowboys and Indians.
P, CYPRUS

UNDERWEAR ENCOUNTER
A few months ago I was out shopping with my bloke for some naughty new underwear. I was trying on a really sexy bra but needed the straps adjusting. As there was no one else in the changing rooms I asked the shop assistant to help. As she was adjusting the straps she started gently touching my breasts. Feeling horny I turned round, we started kissing and one thing

led to another. With one leg on a stool she gently slid my thong off and started licking me out. After giving me a truly ground-shaking orgasm, we got dressed and walked out. My bloke who was waiting outside was none the wiser!

AMY, SUFFOLK

LADY TAKES DARE

Last month my boyfriend dared me to go to the shops with my mini-vibro in me. I had it in all afternoon, even having an orgasm in McDonald's! But in the next shop, I felt it pop out, slide down my leg and by a miracle lodge in the top of my boot instead of rolling across the floor! The dares continue...

L, TELFORD

MODEL GETS WELL INTO THINGS

I'm a glamour model and the other week went on a shoot, this time at a guy's house. It went really well, with me getting turned on exposing all my bits to the fit photographer, while the

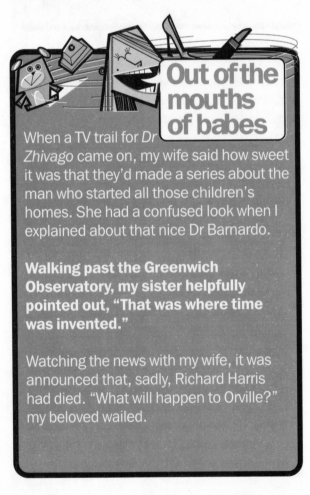

Out of the mouths of babes

When a TV trail for *Dr Zhivago* came on, my wife said how sweet it was that they'd made a series about the man who started all those children's homes. She had a confused look when I explained about that nice Dr Barnardo.

Walking past the Greenwich Observatory, my sister helpfully pointed out, "That was where time was invented."

Watching the news with my wife, it was announced that, sadly, Richard Harris had died. "What will happen to Orville?" my beloved wailed.

house owner looked on with a bulge in his trousers. When all the shots had been done the three of us headed to a nearby pub to unwind. After a little booze I was getting frisky and dying to shag the photographer. So I thought I may as well come out with it. I said to the bloke whose house it was, "I'll give you £20 if you let me and him have use of your bedroom for an hour." He accepted! So we all headed back to his, and me and the snapper disappeared into the guy's room. After some even naughtier photos we had a fantastic sex session. God I love porno shoots!

K, DONCASTER

NOVELTY PARTY LEADS TO BATHTIME FUN

Recently it was my friend's birthday party, and it was decreed that it would be a themed Rubik's Cube party. What this means is that every guest wears one of each of the six colours of the Rubik's Cube and during the night you swap clothes, so by the end of the evening you're in one colour. The idea is that you have to persuade a member of the opposite sex to swap an item of clothing, whether it be trousers, top – or underwear! It promised to be great, sexy fun as we had a mixed crew of good-looking guys and gals. Sure enough, it soon got heated as the clothes were coming off and going on and the drink was flowing. I swapped my red panties for a guy's blue boxers and felt incredibly horny showing him my pussy as we exchanged smalls. I could see from his swelling cock he enjoyed it too! To cut a long story short, a load of us ended up in a big bath together, where I had my pussy licked by a girl with a tongue stud and my tits sucked by some bloke while his brother had a wank over us. A birthday party to remember!

SARAH, LONDON

KNICKERLESS STUDENT TEASES COLLEGE LECTURER

I am a history student and for a bet with my girlfriends I agreed to wear a short shirt and no panties for a full day. I attended my morning lecture which was being taken by our particularly hunky tutor. I sat near the front and, very briefly, kept opening my legs a small

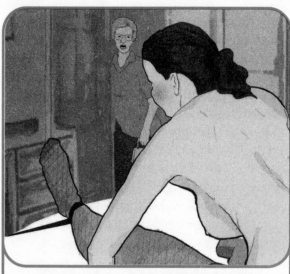

Mum walks in on kinky sex

When I was still living at home and my parents were on holiday, I took the opportunity to get kinky with my boyfriend. Trouble is my folks arrived home a couple of days early, and of course I was in bed with my boyfriend at the time. When my mum walked in my bloke was tied spread-eagled to the bed. I was naked and sat on his face as he licked me out, while I played with and sucked his cock. This image alone would have been enough to embarrass most mothers, but he was also wearing a pair of fishnets, a red suspender belt and matching bra. My mother very tactfully withdrew, and went out again with my dad for a few hours. The bizarre thing was that my boyfriend never knew what happened, since I was sat on his face enjoying myself.

ANN, VIA E-MAIL

way. I soon noticed that he kept looking over, unsure whether he was really seeing my pussy or not. This went on for the whole hour – by the end he was a stuttering, flustered wreck! On the way out I gave him a little bonus, giving him a cheeky flash of my arse. Boy, am I a tease!

SARAH, CUMBRIA

PASSIONATE CRIES HEARD ALL AROUND

I was in my new boyfriend's flat and things started to get really hot and steamy on his leather sofa. Soon it escalated into raunchy, filthy sex and as always I got really noisy. After we finished, the phone rang. He answered it and started laughing hysterically. The intercom to his flat had broken and when his mate rang the buzzer my passionate screams were broadcast to the street outside. When a shocked old lady walked past he proudly announced, "That's my mate doing that, that is!" I still haven't lived it down!

SUZANNE, CARDIFF

HOUSE GUEST OUTSTAYS WELCOME

During the summer I had one of my male "friends" staying with me for a few days. I already had a boyfriend, so my mum was not in the least suspicious. One night me and him went out for a few drinks and, sure enough, on the way home had a little fool around before reaching my house. We went up to my room where things started to get heated. I ripped off his boxer shorts, rolled up my tiny skirt and straddled him on the bed. Next thing I knew I heard my bedroom door open. He threw me off him, pulled the blankets over him and pretended to be asleep before my mum came in to ask where all the noise was coming from. I told her that my friend had drunk a little too much and was feeling sick. Then, before I could do anything, she whipped back the bed clothes. She found him naked from the waist down with a throbbing hard-on wearing nothing but a strawberry-flavoured condom. Oh dear. He went home first thing the next morning.

SHEENA, VIA E-MAIL

PADDLERS GIVE GREAT SHOW

Me and my boyfriend Lee will have sex pretty much anywhere. So when we went on holiday to Spain we thought we'd try it in the sea. We figured that if we went out far enough people wouldn't see. Anyway, as we were fucking and were both really turned on, I heard people's voices. I turned around and saw that we weren't the only two turned on – there were two lads wanking while watching us. Incredibly, they were obviously more embarrassed than us, as they then swam off so we could finish what we'd started!

VICKY, BRISTOL

ROMAN STRIP-SEARCH LEADS TO AIRPORT FRISKINESS

My boyfriend and I were returning from a naughty weekend in Rome, having to get up early for our flight. Scrambling to get clothes on and still a bit drunk from the night before, I just put on what I'd had on then, a black mini, black boots and a top. We made it in time but going through passports noticed the Italian police giving me a good eyeing up. Luckily, the boyfriend found this funny until I was pulled to one side and taken off to a room where I was searched. The fact that it was two gorgeous Italian policemen stopped me from protesting. One said they were looking for drugs, a feeble excuse I thought and let them carry on. Before long, I was stood in black boots, panties and bra with four hands exploring everywhere you can imagine. I emerged 20 minutes later, red-faced but very horny! On the flight back, I told my guy what had happened and as we had a row to ourselves, he was soon getting his first mile-high hand-job.

LARA, VIA E-MAIL

TEEN GETS EDUCATED

When I was 17 I went out with a boy of about the same age. One day I went to his house but he wasn't in, so his older sister invited me in to wait. She got some wine out and we giggled about girly stuff, and when I mentioned I was worried about being a crap kisser she suggested we kiss. I decided what the heck! She said it was great and could we try it again. She ran her hands all over my body and then squeezed my boobs! Soon in our underwear, she took my hand to lead me upstairs. My heart was pounding, but I was also dripping from all the foreplay. Upstairs, she began by going down on me. But just then the cupboard door flew open revealing a man with his trousers round his ankles and a huge hard-on. He also had a video camera in his other hand. I screamed and my boyfriend's sister jumped up and yelled at him. It turned out he was her boyfriend and he was meant to be just watching, not videoing. After a row they started kissing and then looked at me – I couldn't take my eyes off his huge knob! They both got on the bed and he started kissing me while she was busy fingering herself. He put his cock in my mouth, and she began licking me out. I had an amazing orgasm and after he came in my mouth she kissed me and swallowed it all. We ended up having sex another four times, and I got a taste of everything. It made me realise what a crap shag my bloke really was!

C, CRAWLEY

SEX TOYS OFFERED FOR TESTING

Before last Christmas I went on a shopping trip in Cologne with my mum. We were in a market when we spotted a sex shop, so in true FHM fashion we thought, Why not? We duly went inside, only to find that half the shop was discounted goods – because they were second-hand! We found this out because as I was looking at some of the sex toys the shop assistant asked me if I would like to "sample one of them"! I asked her what she meant and was told, "You can go in that room and have a try. There are some wipes to clean it after you've used it"! I promptly grabbed my mum and we left in fits of laughter.

LUCY, VIA E-MAIL

Out of the mouths of babes

At a party, we were playing "Six Degrees Of Kevin Bacon" – connecting any movie to the eponymous film star through six actors or less. My girlfriend set me a tough one: *Footloose*. Starring, er, Kevin Bacon.

Ladies' Confessions

ACCIDENTAL THREESOME GETS TOO MUCH FOR SOME

It was one of the most drunken nights that me and my best friend have ever had, and when we got home we carried on drinking, getting louder and louder until my boyfriend came down complaining that we were making too much noise. Trouble is, he hadn't done the front of his boxers up and everything he had was on display. At this point my sloshed, turned-on mate suggested a threesome, so, feeling well up for it – and the fact that my boyfriend's dick had just gone up faster than a Frenchman's hands – we were off. All was going well until, just as me and my mate were pleasuring him orally, he coughed and farted and came all at the same time. Both of us just fell about laughing as he stormed off.

TESSA, VIA E-MAIL

Out of the mouths of babes

Watching *Executive Decision* with my girlfriend, we came to the part where the two planes were hooked together. After popping out to answer a call of nature, I asked her what had happened in my absence. "The pilot ejaculated," she answered innocently.

My father bought an antique wireless radio. Showing it to my girlfriend of the time, he explained that it needed to warm up, before tuning it in to Radio One. "Oh my God!" exclaimed my woman, bewitched. "It plays modern music!"

Watching a TV ad for Durex where men dressed up as sperm followed a bloke around, one of my female friends piped up: "What have spring onions got to do with condoms?"

ROAD TRIP GETS SQUIDGY

The annual Bank Holiday weekend break to Skegness was upon us and my mum, dad, my boyfriend and myself were cooped up inside the family Astra. After about four hours of non-stop driving I was rudely awoken by my man's erect love length digging into my waist. Checking in front I found my ma was dozing and dad engrossed in Five Live, so proceeded to resolve the "problem" in no time. However, not getting caught in the act wasn't enough to satisfy my lover's fantasies and being the daredevil that he is, he tapped my mum on the shoulder and asked her if she had a spare tissue…

JO, HIGH WYCOMBE

TWINS HAVE FUN

I have an identical twin sister. We are exactly the same in every way: looks, personality, laugh, smile, voice, everything. One night we thought we'd play a trick on her boyfriend. We swapped clothes – even underwear – and I went to meet her fella pretending to be her. She was meant to come out later and surprise him, but texted and cancelled. He was none the wiser so I ended up staying out and getting stupidly drunk with him. One thing led to another and before I knew it we were at his flat shagging away. He told me it was the best and filthiest sex we'd had "so far"!

JEN, VIA E-MAIL

SUMMER HEAT DAMPENED

Last summer I had a barbecue. My boyfriend and I had been together for seven months, but I'd recently started seeing his sexier best mate, so invited him along rather than my boyfriend. But annoyingly, my boyfriend turned up! He started sulking when he saw his mate there so I decided to "cheer him up" before getting his best mate back for a proper shag after my boyfriend had left. Once everyone started leaving, my boyfriend tempted me into a corner in the garden and ripped off my skirt. He started fumbling with my clit but wasn't getting it right, while all the time my bladder was aching. I was still desperate to come so I helped him out by guiding him to the right spot. But this

Al fresco couple bothered

The sunny weather inspired me and my man to track down new places to have sex, so we went for a cycle with the intention of finding a cool spot to get down to it. Just feeling the bike seat on my pussy was making me horny, so when we saw a field sloping up from the cycle track we knew we had to get shagging right there. Kneeling down near a fence I pulled out Tom's hard cock and began sucking away, grabbing at his balls. I then ordered him to screw me from behind. Halfway through the hardest fucking of my life I heard a voice that wasn't my boyfriend's. Some scabby farmer guy had tapped Tom on the shoulder and said: "I'm really horny watching you. Just wondering if you need another cock." Mortified doesn't come close…

NATALIE, BRISTOL

unfortunately relaxed me so much I pissed on his hand! He was well pleased – until I told him it was wee! I'm now with his best mate.

J, SUSSEX

SHOPPER RELIEVES BOREDOM

One Bank Holiday Monday my parents dragged me around a furniture superstore. Bored to tears I sat myself down and let them get on with it. It turned out the chair I'd chosen had a remote control and after pushing a few buttons it began to quietly vibrate. One turn of a dial later and the vibrating sped up – plus I had my legs crossed and a tight pair of jeans on. In a few minutes I was having an orgasm while the rest of middle England shopped around me totally unawares.

JJ, MERSEYSIDE

LADY PENS GRATITUDE

I was recently reading FHM's High Street Honeys booklet and as I'm secretly bi-curious, started to feel really horny. As I was all alone in the house I started to play with myself. I came three times in a row and by the time I'd finished my fingers were soaking! So I just wanted to say thanks FHM for the best wank of my life!

SAMANTHA, MANCHESTER

WHO DONE IT?

Last summer, I went back to this guy's flat for some no-strings sex. After about 15 minutes of shagging he moaned as he blew his load and proceeded to roll over and go to sleep. As I was drunk I didn't complain and joined him in catching 40 winks. The next day as I woke I was greeted with the most disgusting smell. To my horror I realised that during shagging the night before I had shit myself! I nipped off to the bathroom to clean myself up. When I returned I gently rolled my one-night stand over to the other side of the bed. When he woke to find what he believed to be his bedtime mess he came over all embarrassed and apologetic. I assured him it was fine and then saw myself to the door.

RACHEL, NEWCASTLE

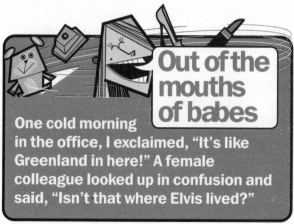

Out of the mouths of babes

One cold morning in the office, I exclaimed, "It's like Greenland in here!" A female colleague looked up in confusion and said, "Isn't that where Elvis lived?"

Ladies' Confessions

NIGHTLIFE IS BLINDING

I was out for a drink with some mates in Manchester when this horny guy started chatting me up. It wasn't long before we were rushing to find a quiet spot to get down to some frisky business. Kissing and groping, we both made a grab for each other's rude bits. He pushed my head down so I would blow him, but I just started off by wanking him slowly and playing with his balls. It was all going well but suddenly he creamed into my right eye! To hide the shame, I had to pretend to my friends that I was crying because I'd hurt my foot rather than simply being jizzed on.

PHOEBE, MANCHESTER

CUNNING PLAN

My fella and I were on the verge of breaking up although we still lived together. One night I was out on the tiles with my friends and met up with a hunk I knew from the gym. Things between gym hunk and me started hotting up and I thought, "What the hell?" and took him back to my house. We got down and dirty on my bed when I heard a taxi pull up, and to my horror, it was the ex. Panic ensued but as the ex had no key, he obviously couldn't get in. So, he started trying to prise open the window while ringing my mobile. Crafty as I am though, I thought up a plan; I rang his mobile and when he answered he started shouting, "Open the door, I'm outside!" to which I replied, "I'm at my friend's house and can't get a taxi home, walk down and meet me halfway." Bearing in mind this is four in the morning, the ex then dutifully walked away from the house to my friend's to make sure I got home safely. My gym hunk and I got dressed and left the house, he flagged down a taxi, dropped me off near the friend's house I'm meant to be at and I then proceeded to walk up to meet my ex. Genius!

NICOLA, VIA E-MAIL

CAR TROUBLE

I was at home with my boyfriend, feeling very horny. Unfortunately my mum was also in. So we had the idea of going for a little drive! It didn't take me long to begin sucking on his

Out of the mouths of babes

My current girlfriend's sister had a summer job in a department store. I asked if that meant she got a discount. "No," my girl replied, "although she does only pay three-quarters of the price."

A female friend of mine recently moved into a house where the fridge didn't work, so her dad bought her some dried milk. "How do I use this with cornflakes?" she asked me. "Do I sprinkle it on?" Brilliant.

My Scottish mate had just become a dad, and joked that his little boy would probably end up with his huge conk and flat feet. "Will he inherit your accent, or will he speak English like your wife?" queried my girlfriend, in all seriousness.

cock. The pleasure was so great for my boyfriend, he just couldn't control his speed and drove through a speed camera without even noticing. Two weeks later, his mother received a letter with a fine for speeding and included was the picture from the speed camera with my head clearly sucking his lolly!

DIPTESH, VIA E-MAIL

SUSPENDERS CAUSE SUSPENSE

After receiving a rather sexy bra and thong set from my boyfriend for Christmas, I decided to supplement it with the matching suspender belt. The ensemble produced the desired effect on my boyfriend and we both had a very satisfying night together. But about a week later, feeling a little broke, I decided to return the suspender belt in order to raise some extra cash. As I removed it from the bag, the efficient shop assistant asked if it had been worn. "Oh no," I responded confidently, "it's just that it's

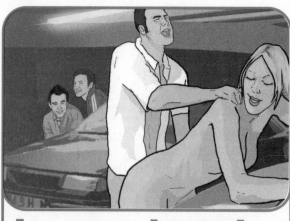

Lovers head underground

After a fantastic night out with my boyfriend and his mates, my bloke and I decided to sneak off to a nearby underground car park for a quick shag. When we got there I took off my dress and stood there wearing nothing but a pair of black hold-ups and a smile. My boyfriend then gave me the ride of my life, his arse going like a fiddler's elbow, with me bent over a car. After he shot his load all over my arse he shouted, "Who's the daddy?" He then said his mates would never believe him if he told them what we'd done. Just as he said that his mates jumped out from behind the wall and shouted, "Next!" He was livid and apologised all the way home for his mates' perverted behaviour. So then I decided there was no way I could tell him that it was me who told them they could watch...

TRACY, VIA E-MAIL

completely unsuitable." Then, to my horror, under the bright store lights I spotted a wiry, spiralling pubic hair standing to attention in the sheer net fabric. Beginning to glow, I stood my ground hoping she wouldn't notice. It wasn't until the assistant used her long, perfectly manicured nail to scratch away at a newly visible, white crusty patch that I cut my losses, grabbed the lingerie and ran out!

ANON, BRISTOL

GONDOLA GETS STEAMY

Last Christmas my bloke and I were snowboarding in Austria. One afternoon a whiteout forced us to leave the mountain early and we got a gondola all to ourselves. Not ones to waste an opportunity like this we started snogging as soon as the doors closed. It wasn't long till his board pants were around his ankles and his cock was in my mouth. It wasn't until he'd finished emptying his load that we noticed the gondola had a CCTV camera. Sure enough, as we left the gondola we were greeted by three sniggering lifties, the last of whom shook my boyfriend's hand…

LIZ, VIA E-MAIL

DANGER: ODD FEMALE

One of my secret sex fantasies has always been to get kidnapped for a steamy sex session. I mentioned this to my boyfriend, but never thought he would act on it. Then one day I was walking down to the supermarket when a van pulled up and a masked man grabbed me and dragged me inside. Not knowing what was happening, I started screaming. Then the man let me know he was actually my fella and he wanted sex. I felt myself getting wet almost instantly and we started ripping off each other's clothes. A few moments later he was taking me from behind and I was screaming to make him go even harder and deeper. Just when we were about to climax, the door was violently opened and we were both dragged out. Apparently someone saw what happened and called the police, who thought I was being raped. I've

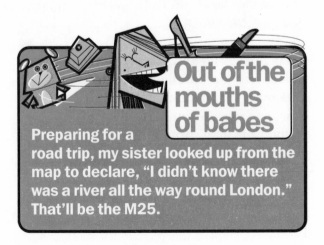

Out of the mouths of babes

Preparing for a road trip, my sister looked up from the map to declare, "I didn't know there was a river all the way round London." That'll be the M25.

never been so embarrassed in my life, but
fortunately the police laughed about it. And I
made sure my ex came around later to finish off
what he'd started.

LOTTE, VIA E-MAIL

HELL HATH NO FURY…

After finding out the man I was with had been
unfaithful I was – unsurprisingly – pissed off.
I went round to his place while he was at work to
get my stuff and found his very dishy flatmate
shirtless and looking very horny. I decided my
revenge should be to shag said flatmate on my
ex's bed, leaving the mess for him to clean up.
When my ex found out, he trashed my car, so
I decided to ring the police to inform them of
the little illegal plants growing in his basement!
Revenge is sweet.

WILLOW, LONDON

PIERCED BLISS

One day, for no apparent reason other than
I was bored, I decided to go and get my clit hood
pierced. I put on a nice lacy thong and off I
went. I got to the studios and it all went without
a hitch. Afterwards it felt really sensitive, plus it
didn't help that my jeans were a tad tight. The
constant rubbing was seriously turning me on,
but it was only when I got on the bus that things
really started happening. It was a bit old and
rickety and the seat I chose happened to be over
a wheel. About halfway home, the vibrations
were really getting me hot and bothered. I was
having an orgasm on the bus, and it's sooo hard
to keep quiet doing that! Let's just say, it was the
best bus ride of my life, and I love that piercing!

REBECCA, VIA E-MAIL

TWISTED SISTERS

I thought it would a nice idea to surprise my
fella, so I went out and bought some bondage
gear and a vibro. When I got back home I was
really horny, and when I got talking to my sister,
we decided to devise a little game. When my
bloke got home I took him up to our bedroom
while my sister hid. I tied him up to the bed
naked, blindfolded him, then started to give
him oral. Just as he was about to come I stopped

and told him to wait a moment. I moved out of the way and my sister came in with some whipping cream, which she dripped all over his body and slowly licked off. She worked her way down and begun giving him oral until he exploded. She then crept out of the room, which is when I returned and finished the night off for him. He'll never ever know that he got a double helping that night!

SOPHI, VIA E-MAIL

SEASON'S GREETINGS

Over the Christmas period I was going through a bad patch as I'd just split from my boyfriend and during the last two months of our relationship we hadn't had any sex at all. Come Christmas Eve I was sitting in my parents' home all alone. The artificial Christmas tree was looking rather inviting, so with myself feeling sexually frustrated and gagging for it, I grabbed the tree and turned it on its side, removing the Angel to reveal a smooth plastic top. Then I slowly inserted the top of the tree into my vagina and pleasured myself. And to be honest it was the best Christmas present I've ever had.

JJ, SUNDERLAND

BACK DOOR CONFUSION

My husband has been pestering me to let him pop my little brown cherry for three years now and last week I finally agreed to anal sex. That evening he was lying on the bed waiting, so I began by massaging him. He loved it when I started kneading his bum cheeks and didn't even protest when I slipped a finger in. The next thing he felt after I had readied him was the head of a strap-on! I gave him a thorough pounding which he eventually enjoyed. The only drawback was he walked like John Wayne for two days. I guess it was his fault for not asking which way round the anal was going to be going!

SH, GLOUCESTERSHIRE

CHANGING ROOM CHANCER

I'm the captain of a girls' hockey team and last week a hunky male was standing in for our usual coach who was injured. Before practice

I popped into the male changing room to discuss team selection, little expecting to see the new guy lathered up in the shower. I gasped with excitement as he turned to face me, revealing his impressive manhood. Implausible as it sounds, but within minutes I was bent over a nearby table with my arse in the air. My pleated skirt was up, my lacy knickers were down and his big, stiff cock was inside me. He unhooked my bra and began fondling my tits as he pounded my pussy. As he reached climax I span round, knelt down and took his prick in my mouth, gulping down his spunk while

Retro sauce flick becomes cleaning reality

I was lying naked on my bed one morning when I heard a noise outside. I looked out of my window to see the window cleaner climbing up to do his job. The curtains were half open and at first I panicked, but feeling horny I decided to have some fun. I lay back on the bed, spread my legs and started playing with myself. After a few minutes he was still there, with me carrying on pretending I hadn't seen him. My windows are sparkling clean all the time now!

CAROLINE, BLACKPOOL

watching his face contort with pleasure. Who'd have thought playing with a long stick and some balls could be so much fun!

SUSIE, DUNDEE

LADY QUICK TO STRAY

Recently, me, my boyfriend, his best mate and his girlfriend booked a table at a fancy restaurant. A week before the date we got a call from my bloke's mate, saying that he had split from his girlfriend. However, the three of us still went to the restaurant and the evening was going well until my boyfriend got up and shot to the toilet. He came back complaining that he must have a stomach bug. He kept on going to the toilet throughout the night, leaving me and his best mate alone to talk. The mate knew that I fancied him, and he told me he liked me, too. Eventually we left, and while we were on our way home my boyfriend had to stop off at a public loo – that stomach bug again. Drunk and excited by the evening's flirting, I pulled down my boyfriend's mate's trousers and started sucking him off. I did all my tricks to make him come as quickly as possible and when he came, there was a bucketload. Then I heard my boyfriend open the toilet door. I didn't want to swallow the come, so I pretended to be sick. My boyfriend comforted me all the way home, but what he didn't know was that I had just given head to his best friend!

ANON, NEWMARKET

A SORT OF REVENGE

One night I was meant to meet my now ex at a pub which just happens to be in a sleazy part of town. It was his birthday and he was there with his mates as usual. I dressed myself up to the nines and went to meet him but by the time I got there he was pissed and being a prick. Not in the mood for this I said that I was leaving. I left the pub and was walking up the street when a car pulled up beside me (and at this stage I would have done anything to get back at my boyfriend for not giving a shit about me). The window rolled down and the man asked me if I was new to the area, and then it clicked that he thought I was a prostitute! I felt a little tingle in my knickers and gave him the impression that I was. He asked me did I want to get in? I duly obliged and we had some wicked sex back at his – and as a parting present I left him with my naughty little knickers! That'll teach my fella.

ANON, VIA E-MAIL

FHM HELPS OUT

Last night me and my boyfriend had the most amazing sex session! There was come in my hair, come on my tits and, of course, come in my pussy. Know what set us off? Him taking snaps of me in panties for your High Street Honeys competition. Cheers FHM!

VICKY, ESSEX

Out of the mouths of babes

Talking about a pet for our new flat, I suggested a tortoise. My flatmate pointed out that tortoises hibernate for half the year. "Why not get two, then?" my girlfriend chipped in.

BALLOONS COVER JIGGERY

After enjoying a birthday meal out with my boyfriend, his friends and my parents left the restaurant and boarded the minibus we'd hired with lots of red balloons the staff had given me as a gift. It proved tricky to fit them on board but after some rearrangement we all got on. My man and I squeezed onto the back seat, hidden from everyone behind the curtain of balloons. Soon things got a bit steamy when my bloke started caressing me under my skirt. With nobody able to see what we were doing he hitched aside my knickers and I sat on his stiff cock. Our friends were oblivious as they chatted away to us – we did well to reply as things came to a head...

HEIDI, SOUTHSEA

SEXY PLAN SPOILED BY COPPERS

One night I thought I'd give my work-stressed boyfriend a treat by indulging him in one of his fantasies, going to his wearing my full-length black coat and nothing else. Getting-ready time reduced, I jumped in my car and set off to his. Disaster! I saw blue flashing lights in my mirror. I pulled over, praying that the lecture could be administered through the window. This wasn't the case, as the two young policemen asked me to step out the car. Trying to button my coat up while getting out of the car proved difficult, with the officers getting great views of all my naughty bits. Unsurprisingly, they were more interested in where I was off to "on such a chilly night", than giving me a ticking off. The embarrassment!

JOANNA, VIA E-MAIL

Ladies' Confessions

MILE HIGHERS SEDUCE STEWARDESS

My bloke and I are keen travellers – and happily also sex experimenters. We recently flew back from the United States and got chatting to our fantastically sexy stewardess, deliberately steering the conversation towards sex and threesomes. At around midnight, most of the passengers were sound asleep so the three of us met up in the rear galley. After some lingering kisses to break the ice we started to really go for it. Whilst my fella was busy enjoying her fantastic tits, I rode up her tight skirt and peeled off her thong. After a good ten minutes of three-way action we were busted by none other than the clearly gay purser, him catching his team-mate with my boyfriend's cock in her mouth and a couple of my fingers inside her. She was reprimanded and we made the Washington Press. I've kept the newspaper as a souvenir – and of course the thong.

CHARLOTTE, KENT

Out of the mouths of babes

I was telling my girlfriend that I had a mate running the London marathon, and that he was planning to participate in the Belfast one too. "Is that longer than London's?" she asked.

Reading an article on Princess Di, my girl came to a part about "her brother, Charles Spencer". "I thought her brother's name was Earl," she said.

My lady and I were having a Chinese when we heard people talking about being born in the year of the rat. Asked if she knew what year she'd been born in, she said, "'Course, 1978."

NURSE 'ASSISTS' SPERM DONOR

I work as a nurse in a sperm bank, which is pretty dull most of the time, but has its moments. Recently this sexy guy came in and I proceeded to flirt with him outrageously, asking him questions like, "How often do you wank?" I felt myself getting wet down below as he said things like, "Yeah, I really love wanking over tall, sexy blondes." Shortly I led him to one of our rooms with his little cup. At first I left him there by himself but the thought of him pleasing himself made me even more wet and I couldn't contain myself. I practically ran into the room and said something like, "Thought it'd be best to give you a hand..." Straight away we started kissing and he ran his hands all over my body, stopping between my legs. I climaxed within seconds, then dropped to my knees and gave him a blow-job. When he was finished, I spat the contents into his cup – after all, he was there to donate!
LOUISE, DUBLIN

CHEAT PLAYS RISKY GAME

Sex with my bloke was getting a bit boring, so I started an affair with someone from the office. After a while we got more daring and started doing it in our bed while my man was out. One Sunday my lover and I were getting frisky when I heard the door open! My bloke's footie game had been called off and he had come home. To his surprise there I was in bed, horny and dressed up in my schoolies! My lover was hiding in the wardrobe so I said to my bloke that it was about time he got home and why didn't he get down there and give me a good licking! While he was busy under the duvet my lover had a chance to sneak out but thought it'd be a giggle to wave his cock in my face. What the hell, I played along for a bit, keeping my boyfriend's head firmly on my cooch while I sucked my lover's cock!
LUCY, VIA E-MAIL

PRIVATE DANCER TREAT

I used to dance naked in a club, partly because I needed the cash, and also because I enjoy getting my kit off. One evening a couple asked

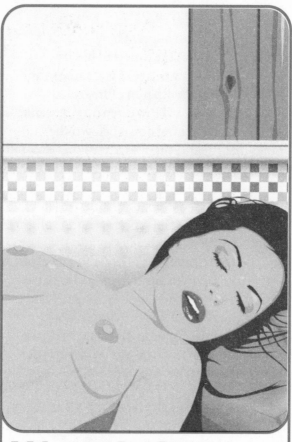

Water babe gets audience

Last summer, when my parents were away, I went to house-sit as they have a pool. I was all on my own one sunny day so I decided to take off my bikini, as it's lovely swimming naked. After a few laps I had a sunbathe on the Lilo. A short time later, feeling a bit frisky, I started to rub myself and got more and more into it. As the Lilo floated about and turned round, I glanced up and in front of me were three of my parents' neighbours and ALL their kids. Mum hadn't told me she'd told them to "pop round for a swim any time"! The worse thing was after I'd got out the pool, one of the women who was quite old and pretty minging, whispered to me, "I don't blame you, love, when I'm on my own, I have a little fiddle, rub 'n' tickle while doing the laundry." I felt sick to the stomach.
CAROLINE, BERKSA

Out of the mouths of babes

On a trip to a park, my wife and I joined some schoolkids for a tour of the cow fields, where she raised her hand and asked, "Why do all of your cows have girls' names?"

During a school trip to a small island a few years ago my sister and I ate our packed lunches together, which attracted loads of greedy birds. "How did they get to the island?" my sis blurted out.

Driving the old girl down the A5, a motorbike with German registration went flying past. "I wonder if that's left, or right-hand drive?" mused my mum.

me for a private dance in the back. The club was strict on this, so I had to say no, but they offered me 200 quid, so I said I'd go to their house at the end of the night if they were still interested. Sure enough I went along and was soon on all fours getting a good seeing to, with a mouthful of cock and being shagged from behind by a woman with a dildo! She had the most filthy mouth I'd ever heard, which made me even hornier. They screwed me until I was exhausted – it was mind-blowing! I don't dance any more, but I did move in with them two months ago, (rent free!) and we have the most amazing sex sessions ever.

JANE, VIA E-MAIL

DARE NOT TRUTH

A few months ago I was having a party at my house because my parents had gone out and weren't expected home till the early hours. Me and my mates were all getting drunk and so we decided to play Truth Or Dare. Everyone was choosing truth and it was getting boring, so I asked my boyfriend to think of a good dare to

give me. When it came to my turn I chose a dare and it was for me to get it on with my best female mate. So we were in the middle of the room having a good snogging, me with my tits out, when suddenly all went quiet. I stood up to see my parents standing at the door! I have never been allowed a party since, and they think I am in denial about being a lesbian because I am still with my boyfriend.
J, LANCASHIRE

SWIMMING POOL SAUCE

I was on holiday with friends, and we were having the time of our lives getting well and truly bladdered. One booze-soaked night, we decided to go skinny-dipping in the hotel pool. One of the guys in our party was obviously enjoying the sight of me and the other sexy girls a little too much, because he had the stiffest cock I'd seen all

Out of the mouths of babes

Watching the news about the Ark Royal departing for the Gulf, the commentator said that the ship was carrying, amongst other weaponry, Merlin anti-submarine helicopters. "Does that mean they fly underwater?" asked my girlfriend.

While taking the last of her three daily inhalers, my girlfriend exclaimed, "I seem to spend half my life just breathing in!"

Playing 20 Questions during a long train journey, my girlfriend had to guess I was thinking of Freddie Mercury. She couldn't even work out what industry he was in, so as a not-so-subtle hint I started playing with my Walkman. "I get it!" she squealed. "Is it the man who invented headphones?"

Cadet utilises what's to hand

When I was 18, I was in the Air Cadet Corps and once every few months we'd all go away on camp. I'd been in since I was 13 and had made my way through most of the lads so I thought it was time I took my turn with the ladies. Soon after the girls had rolled into their billets after lights out, me and my mate were feeling rather frustrated and started kissing for a laugh. Soon we became more horny and were playing with each other's beautiful tits and pussies. I reached around the room looking for something to frig her with and laid my hands on a military torch. I slid it into her tight cooch, then played with my tits in front of the beam, giving her a "breast shadow play" while she was in ecstasy. Ace!

LEANNA, SHEFFIELD

month! Feeling drunk and horny, me and the girls decided to surprise him by diving underwater and sucking hard on his hot tool. Needless to say, he was thoroughly appreciative and shot his juicy load all over the pool! Feeling indebted to me (having been the last to suck him off) he paid me back by giving me the best bum-bang I've ever had! When I walked to the pool the next day (with some difficulty!) I was horrified to discover the come still floating in the water. Yuk!

KIRSTY, NEWCASTLE

Marines get eyeful

I am a serving member of the RAF, working in the stores department of the RAF transit and holiday centre in Southern Oman. About four weeks ago, a group of about 80 royal marines were staying at the camp, having returned from Afghanistan, and at night frequented the bar for several hours. One night I went along, had several drinks too many and proceeded to flirt with a fit and tanned marine. Wanting to check out the stamina and endurance marines are famed for, we went off to a quiet, dark tent. Soon he was shagging me silly, with me bent over a lads' camp bed. Then I looked over my shoulder to see three other marines, on their camp beds at the other side of the tent, watching us go at it like rabbits, masturbating furiously. I felt so horny and dirty I gave them a wink and carried on with my beasting!

CARRIE, LIVERPOOL

CLEANER'S BIG ENTRANCE

After a night of amazing sex with a guy I picked up at the Student Union, I got the usual bout of mid morning horniness. My guy started taking me in the ass while massaging my tits. Then, just as he was about to come, his sexy 29-year-old cleaner came barging into the room, with my man just managing to whip his cock out in time. The cleaner then calmly proceeded to slip his still hard cock in her mouth while I looked on, watching as she milked his man juice into her

My ex once got a letter from her bank, informing her she was badly overdrawn. "I'm not!" she wailed, waving her chequebook. "Look – I've got loads of cheques left."

When I asked the woman behind the newsagent's counter recently whether they had any Fisherman's Friends, she made a beeline for the magazine rack. "I can't see it here – but we've got Angler's Week, Trout And Salmon…"

When my girlfriend was learning to drive, she was asked, "What do you need to watch for falling off the trees in autumn?" Her reply: "Squirrels." She's a copper, by the way.

After hearing that the Pentagon had been attacked on 9/11, my girl assured me that Sheffield would be next on the hit list. "We've got the Octagon…" she explained.

mouth. Little did she know where it had been, and she was so surprised when my guy threw her out of his room when she tried to kiss him!
PAULA, VIA E-MAIL

UNDERACHIEVER LOSES DATE

I was shagging this bloke who I just met, back at his place. He really was the shittest lay I'd ever had – the guy was barely moving, flopped on top of me like a limp fish. Five minutes in I realised I couldn't cope with another minute of this, so I told him to get out of me because I was desperate for a wee. He rolled off and I got out of bed, slipped my dress on and left the room. Then I went straight to the lounge, picked up my bag and shoes and headed for the front door. See ya!
NAOMI, HARROGATE

Ladies' Confessions

NEWCOMER PROVES CREDENTIALS

I'd just started a new job and there was a "Welcome to the team," night out. Everyone got absolutely hammered on shots and started performing their party tricks – doing impressions or juggling with the ashtrays. So for mine, I got my tits out, right in front of my thirtysomething boss, and showed all my new colleagues how I could get them in my own mouth. It was the shortest job I ever had.
HELENE, EAST LONDON

COUPLE PERFORM FOR GATHERING

It was a works summer ball and I met this guy from the other office. We got on like a house on fire – due to the fact that I'd been downing red wine all night and had my beer goggles well and truly in place. It was nearing the end of the night when I challenged him that he dare not shag me outside. But he dared, so off we went. There was a big swing in the grounds out front, he sat down and I hitched up my posh dress and climbed aboard. There I was, bouncing up and down on him, just as an announcement was made inside the venue for everyone to start making their way onto the waiting coaches to go home. We ended up surrounded by cheering, pissed blokes, asking if they could have a go, too!
LISA, NEWCASTLE

Out of the mouths of babes

On The Life Of Mammals, David Attenborough closed with: "Next week the story of the apes, and how one large primate took over the world." My watching girlfriend replied with, "Who's that, King Kong?"

After telling my mum that a mate was on holiday in Kuala Lumpur, she replied, "Aren't they the little people in Charlie And The Chocolate Factory?"

WARD ENJOYS SOUND EFFECTS

When I was 17 I was going out with a man ten years older than me who'd ended up breaking his leg in a motorbike accident. I went to hospital, pulled the curtains around us and without saying a word, gave him the best blow-job I'd ever performed then left feeling as if I was the biggest temptress in the world. Only looking back do I realise that the rest of the ward would have heard every slurp and smack of my lips.

LOUISA, SURREY

LOTION CAUSES DISCOMFORT

I'd been seeing my boyfriend for about two years when I found out the double-crossing bastard had been cheating on me with some woman from his office. So one night I invited him round to my flat, got the candles out, put the romantic music on and suggestively lured him into a massage. I'd got hold of my male flatmate's Deep Heat lotion and started rubbing it seductively onto his knob. His screams haunt me even today.

SARA, EDINBURGH

DINNERTIME SHENANIGANS END ABRUPTLY

I went out for a meal with my boyfriend and his great-looking best mate, Gareth. I was next to my man while the best mate sat opposite, so I slipped my shoes off and started massaging his balls with my toes. Then my boyfriend piped up, "Gareth, why are you stroking my leg?" Gareth's jaw dropped, and the rest of the meal was eaten in silence. I mean, what could the poor boy reply? "Sorry, mate. I was trying to grope your bird's inner thigh!"

HAYLEY, DERBY